Solution-Focused Counseling
in Middle and High Schools

John J. Murphy

AMERICAN
COUNSELING
ASSOCIATION

SOLUTION-FOCUSED COUNSELING IN MIDDLE AND HIGH SCHOOLS

10 9 8 7 6 5 4 3

American Counseling Association
5999 Stevenson Avenue
Alexandria, VA 22304

Director of Acquisitions
Carolyn Baker

Director of Publishing Systems
Michael Comlish

Copyeditor
Annette Van Deusen

Cover Design
Cassidy Design

Library of Congress Cataloging-in-Publication Data
Murphy, John J. (John Joseph), 1955–
    Solution-focused counseling in middle and high schools / John J. Murphy.
       p.   cm.
    Includes bibliographical references and index.
    ISBN 1-55620-170-2 (alk. paper)
    1. Counseling in middle school education—United States—Case studies.   2. Counseling in secondary education—United States—Case studies.   3. Solution-focused therapy—United States—Case studies.   4. Problem-solving therapy—United States—Case studies.
I. Title.
LB1620.5.M83   1997
373.14—dc21
                                                                                    97-5511
                                                                                         CIP

Dedication

To my wife, Debbie, and my children, Tom, Erin, and Maura, thank you for your love and patience. To my mother, Mary Murphy, thank you for your continued encouragement and example.

Table of Contents

PART ONE

*Introduction to Solution-Focused Counseling:
Empirical and Therapeutic Influences*

PART TWO

Steps and Strategies of Solution-Focused Counseling

PART THREE

Troubleshooting and Getting Started

Preface

Middle and high school counselors are asked for their assistance in resolving school problems on a daily basis. Failing grades. Unacceptable classroom behavior. School truancy. The list seems to grow each year, as does the need for practical and effective problem-solving approaches that are responsive to the time constraints, large caseloads, and other realities of school professionals. *Solution-Focused Counseling in Middle and High Schools* has been written in response to this need.

The real world of school counselors does not provide them the luxury or opportunity to conduct in-depth interviews and interventions for every school problem. When opportunities do occur, they are not at all like traditional counseling sessions where the client and counselor meet for an hour without interruption. During any given school counseling session, it is not uncommon for the phone to ring or for people to knock on the door despite a "Do Not Disturb" sign. School counselors typically have many other duties besides counseling. These duties may include scheduling classes, monitoring the lunchroom, filling in for a teacher, and group testing, to name just a few.

Some counselors give up altogether on counseling because of the many constraints and other duties that pull them away from it. Because schools are not adapted to counseling, counselors must adapt to schools. Although not ideal, effective counseling can occur in the hallway, on the phone, on the playground, in the lunchroom, in the parking lot, and any other time and place that presents itself. *Solution-Focused Counseling in Middle and High Schools* encourages practitioners to seize the moment whenever possible and to make the best use of every counseling opportunity. The book offers hope in the form of a practical, empirically based approach to resolving middle and high school problems.

Solution-focused counseling is a unique method of problem solving that seeks to promote changes in school problems in a very short period of time. Solutions are enhanced by encouraging students, parents, and teachers to discover and apply their own unique resources and strengths to the problem at hand. The respect and utilization of what clients bring to counseling lies at the heart of the solution-focused approach.

Although there are some distinct differences between solution-focused and other counseling approaches, the ideas and strategies in this book can be successfully applied regardless of one's current theoretical orientation or model of practice. Solution-focused counseling offers a unique way of viewing school problems and the people who experience them. In conducting workshops around the country, I have discovered that school professionals find this approach to be very appealing for several reasons:

- It takes the practical position that counseling is more effective when practitioners "do what works" instead of trying to be fancy and complex.
- It is conceptually simple and does not require extensive background or experience in psychology or counseling. This increases its appeal to parents, teachers, and school administrators.
- It focuses on small changes and reasonable goals, which is well-suited to the realities of school counseling.
- It emphasizes strengths, successes, resources, and hope.
- It encourages the acceptance and accommodation of diverse opinions and beliefs.
- It provides numerous strategies and options for those times when nothing else seems to work.
- It makes school counseling a lot more fun and relaxing.

ORGANIZATION AND CONTENTS

Solution-Focused Counseling in Middle and High Schools is organized in three parts. Part One introduces solution-focused counseling by way of a short case study (Chapter 1) and a description of its empirical and clinical influences (Chapters 2 and 3). Short practice exercises are provided at the end of each chapter in the book to help counselors apply solution-focused strategies to their own cases and circumstances.

Part Two describes and illustrates the practical application of this approach to a variety of middle and high school problems. Chapters 4 through 10 address each step in the counseling process from the initial establishment of an effective relationship (Chapter 4) through termination (Chapter 10). Chapter 5 presents specific "interventive" interviewing strategies designed not only to gather information, but to initiate solutions as well. Chapters 6 through 9 describe four avenues of intervention for school problems: utilizing exceptions to the problem (Chapter 6), utilizing other client resources (Chapter 7), changing the doing of the problem (Chapter 8), and changing the viewing of the problem (Chapter 9). Each chapter describes the intervention strategy, then presents several case examples of its application with a variety of actual school problems. Most cases include excerpts from actual counseling sessions. Although these are real cases, the names of the people involved and some of the details have been changed to prevent identification of a specific student, parent, or teacher. I personally served as the counselor on all but two cases in this book ("The Student Who Refused to Read" and "Sweeping the Sidewalk Twice").

Part Three includes two chapters. Chapter 11 provides troubleshooting guidelines to consider when things do not go as planned. This book concludes with Chapter 12, which offers suggestions for putting solution-focused counseling into practice where you work.

This book has been written primarily for school counselors, psychologists, social workers, graduate students in counseling and psychology, and others who provide counseling for middle and high school students. Teachers and school administrators have also found the ideas and strategies of solution-focused counseling to be useful in their work.

TERMINOLOGY

The word *client* is used in this book to describe anyone with whom practitioners work to change a school problem, including students, parents, teachers, and school administrators. The term *counseling* is used to describe any type of work that practitioners do with clients for the purpose of resolving school problems. This includes individual and group sessions with students as well as consultation with parents and teachers. The term *solution* refers to any noticeable improvement in a school problem, not necessarily a complete elimination of it. For the sake of clarity, the term *middle school* is used to refer to grades 6 through 8, and *high school* to grades 9 through 12.

Is this book for you? I invite you to consider the following questions in this regard. *Have you ever. . .*

- tried to convince students that they have a problem when they do not think they have one?
- watched a student's or parent's eyes glaze over as they turn you off during a counseling session?
- felt overly pressured and underqualified when people looked to you as "the expert" with all the answers?
- thought, "This problem could be solved if I could just get the parent or teacher to change"?
- thought, "Is there a simpler way to do counseling?"
- wanted counseling to be more enjoyable?

This book addresses these and similar questions, and presents practical strategies for dealing with them.

To offer feedback on the book or to inquire about training on solution-focused counseling, please contact:

Dr. John Murphy
University of Central Arkansas
Department of Psychology and Counseling
UCA Box 4915
Conway, AR 72035-0001
(501) 450-3193
email: jmurphy@cc1.uca.edu

Acknowledgments

Many of the ideas and strategies of this book are derived from the work of Steve de Shazer and colleagues at the Brief Family Therapy Center (BFTC) in Milwaukee, Wisconsin. These folks have taught me and many others the benefits of keeping it simple and focusing on what works with people instead of what does not. The brief therapy approach of John Weakland and associates at the Mental Research Institute (MRI) in Palo Alto, California, taught me to "do something different" when things are not working and to accommodate people's beliefs instead of trying to change them. These lessons have been immensely helpful in working with "difficult" adolescents. I am also grateful to Barry Duncan, my friend and colleague with whom I have collaborated on several recent projects. Barry directed my postdoctoral training in brief family therapy, and continues to inspire me regarding the possibilities of solutions in the most difficult of cases, and the benefits of trusting in the resources of clients.

I am thankful to my friends and colleagues in the brief therapy consultation group, Cookie Cahill-Flower, Michael Walters, and Bruce Wess, for the many hours of discussion on solution-focused applications in schools. Michael Walters kindly allowed me to describe one of his cases in Chapter 7 ("Sweeping the Sidewalk Twice"). I appreciate the kindness and cooperation of the students, parents, and staff of Covington (Kentucky) Independent Public Schools during my 13 years there.

I am grateful to the University of Central Arkansas for grant funding, and to David Skotko, Chair of the Psychology and Counseling Department, and Jim Bowman, Dean of the College of Education, for their encouragement and support of this book. I am also thankful for my colleagues in the Psychology and Counseling Department. Cindy Carlson and Mark Hubble graciously agreed to review an earlier draft of the book, and made some excellent suggestions for improving it. I appreciate the proofreading assistance of Mandy Rubow Velasquez, Priscilla Handley, Debbie Murphy, and Patricia Burris, and the technical assistance of Tom Murphy on the book's figures. The enthusiastic direction and support of Carolyn Baker, Director of Acquisitions at the American Counseling Association, was very helpful throughout this project.

Lastly, I thank the many students, parents, and teachers with whom I have been privileged to work. As evidenced throughout this book, middle and high school students are the best teachers of what works and does not work in school counseling.

About the Author

John J. Murphy, Ph.D., is an Assistant Professor of Psychology and Counseling at the University of Central Arkansas, where he trains counselors and psychologists. He also maintains a private practice focusing on school problems. Dr. Murphy taught high school for 2 years upon receiving his undergraduate degree in psychology in secondary education. He received his master's degree and Ph.D. in school psychology from the University of Cincinnati, and worked 13 years as a full-time school psychologist in Covington (Kentucky) Public Schools, an urban district with a diverse student population. During that time, he worked extensively with students, parents, and teachers on middle and high school problems.

Dr. Murphy was named Kentucky School Psychologist of the Year in 1992, and was one of five finalists for National School Psychologist of the Year in 1993. He completed postdoctoral training in strategic family therapy, has authored several articles and book chapters on time-limited school counseling, and has previously authored (with Barry L. Duncan) the book *Brief Intervention for School Problems* (Guilford Press). Dr. Murphy is a widely sought speaker who frequently conducts training workshops throughout the country for counselors, psychologists, social workers, teachers, and administrators.

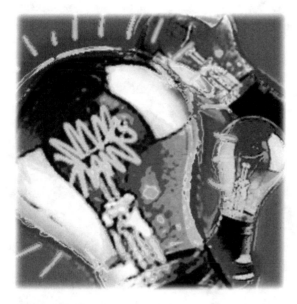

Introduction to Solution-
Focused Counseling:
Empirical and Therapeutic
Influences

The Case of Janet: An Introduction to Solution-Focused Counseling

Force is no remedy.

—John Bright, *On the Irish Troubles*

This chapter introduces solution-focused counseling by way of a short case study involving a high school student named Janet.

GOING NOWHERE FAST

Janet, an 11th-grade student, is referred for school counseling due to on-going behavior and academic problems. Most of the problems occur in math class. Mr. Crawford, the math teacher, describes her as unmotivated, resistant to suggestions, and on her way to failing his class for the second time. When confronted about the problem, Janet shrugs her shoulders and says, "I don't know." Sometimes she says that it's not really her problem, and that everybody should just back off. She reacts similarly when lectured about how important passing grades are to her future. She says that math class is stupid and that her parents and teachers do not understand her. According to her parents, their efforts to reason with her start out okay but usually result in a shouting match.

Enter the school counselor, who is asked by Janet's parents and teachers to meet with her to "make her understand" what she is doing to herself. They also want to know why she refuses to work harder and behave better in school. Janet is called from class to see the counselor. She arrives in the counselor's office, slumps down in the chair, and stares at the floor.

Counseling Session #1: Getting Through to Janet

Counselor: So what I am saying to you is that I can't do it for you, your teachers can't do it for you, and your parents can't do it for you. You are the only one who can make things better for yourself, and things will keep getting worse until you decide to do that. Why are you making this so hard for your-self and everybody else?

Janet: [*shrugs her shoulders*] I don't know. [*slumps even lower in the chair and continues to stare at the floor*]

20 minutes later during the same meeting. . .

Counselor: Janet, we're all trying to help you. If we didn't care about you, we wouldn't be spending this time trying to help you. Do you know what I'm saying?

Janet: Yep.

Counselor: Well, what are you going to do?

Janet: [*shrugs her shoulders*] I don't know.

Counselor: I hope you're going to make a wise choice and turn things around for yourself. Your discipline record is only getting worse, you know.

Janet: Can I go now? The bell is about to ring.

Counselor: Yes, you can go. Please think about what I said. I've seen these things get worse and worse for students. The sooner you change, the better. Okay?

Janet: Yep. [*quickly exits office*]

GOING NOWHERE EVEN FASTER

During the next 2 months, things get worse. Janet's discipline record grows longer and longer, and she is close to receiving an out-of-school suspension. People intensify their position and response to the problem. Mr. Crawford gets on Janet's case even more, sometimes sending her out of class to the discipline office or to in-school suspension. Janet continues to feel misunderstood by her teachers, parents, and school counselor. Her parents keep asking her why she refuses to change, and they call the counselor to report that they have tried everything and are out of ideas. The counselor is frustrated because everyone is looking to counseling for the quick fix.

Counseling Session #2: More of the Same

Janet meets a second time with the counselor, who continues to emphasize the gravity of the situation and the fact that she is headed for serious consequences unless something changes fast.

Counselor: You are digging a hole for yourself that's getting harder and harder to get out of. What's it going to take, Janet?

Janet: Huh?

Counselor: What's it going to take for you to pull yourself out of this mess?

Janet: [*shrugs her shoulders*] I don't know.

Counselor: Do you realize how close you are to being suspended?

Janet: Pretty close.

Counselor: Real close. Are you willing to shape up in Mr. Crawford's class?

Janet: I guess so.

Janet leaves the office, shoulders slumped, to return to class. The counselor heads toward the lunchroom for cafeteria duty, feeling defeated and wondering how to get through to Janet.

A COMMON SCENARIO IN MIDDLE AND HIGH SCHOOLS

The events and circumstances of Janet's situation are familiar to many middle and high school students, parents, teachers, and counselors. The people involved in the problem are stuck in a vicious cycle. The harder they try to resolve the problem, the worse it gets. The worse it gets, the harder they try.

Why is it so easy for middle and high school students, teachers, parents, and counselors to get stuck in the "more of the same" attempts to resolve school problems? More important, what can counselors do to get unstuck, or to avoid such cycles in the first place? These questions are addressed throughout this book.

Many counseling models focus exclusively on the problem. Assessment seeks to clarify the history and presumed causes of the problem, and treatment seeks to remediate the client's deficiencies related to the problem. In school counseling, an exclusive focus on the problem carries with it the implication that there is something wrong or defective about the student.

When adolescent students do not implement a counselor's suggestions, they are typically called uncooperative or resistant. This not only perpetuates the original problem that led to counseling, but often creates two problems where there once was one: the original problem *and* the student's so-called resistance (as if one problem is not enough!). In some approaches, resistance itself becomes the primary counseling issue requiring thorough exploration and intervention. Even if it was possible to force adolescents to change against their will (which is rarely the case), school practitioners do not have the time to carry out extended interventions for every problem presented to them. As evidenced with Janet, attempts to "get through" and to force adolescents into changing often result in a vicious cycle in which the same strategies are used over and over despite their ineffectiveness. This book offers specific techniques and guidelines for dealing with such cycles when they occur, and for avoiding them in the first place.

SOLUTION-FOCUSED COUNSELING: A PRACTICAL ALTERNATIVE

The realities of life in middle and high schools require a counseling approach that is efficient *and* responsive to the unique challenges of working with adolescents. Solution-focused counseling offers great promise as a time-effective, cooperative approach that *shifts the counselor's focus from "what's wrong" to "what's working"* with students. The beliefs, resources, and competencies of students, parents, and teachers are actively sought and applied to the resolution of school problems.

Instead of attempting to push the river in a different direction by breaking through resistances and challenging the student's position, the solution-focused counselor goes with the flow and cooperates with the student's beliefs. Focusing on people's strengths and resources instead of their weaknesses enhances cooperation and leads to more rapid change. The concept of "resistance" is viewed as unnecessary and detrimental to helping people resolve problems (de Shazer, 1984). The reactions of students and others to the problem and to the counselor are viewed as "useful communication" instead of signs of resistance or pathology.

JANET REVISITED: A SOLUTION-FOCUSED APPROACH

Returning to Janet, the following excerpt is from her first meeting with a different counselor. The interview took place during the third quarter of the school year. There are some important differences between this counselor's approach and the prevailing "lecture, probe, and persuade" theme of previous interventions. In the following excerpt, notice how the counselor (a) asks Janet what *she* wants from counseling instead of assuming what her goal is or trying to talk her into a different goal; (b) accepts and cooperates with her view of the problem instead of confronting or challenging it; and (c) invites her to consider what she has already done or is presently doing to help reach her goal, instead of focusing on what she is not doing or on what she is doing wrong. Observe the differences in the way Janet responds during this counseling session as compared to previous sessions.

Counselor: I've already talked to your parents and some of your teachers. What I want to know is what *you* want to see happen with all this school stuff.
Janet: I want to get a better grade in math. Nobody believes me, but I do.
Counselor: Why do you want a better grade?
Janet: I don't want to take this class again for the *third* time. I couldn't handle that.
Counselor: Two times is enough, huh?
Janet: Really.
Counselor: What kind of grade are you making?
Janet: D's and F's.
Counselor: Are D's and F's all right with you, or do you want different grades?
Janet: What do you mean?
Counselor: Well, everybody's different. I've met some students that are okay with getting D's and F's, and others that want A's. So I was wondering what kind of grades you would be satisfied with.
Janet: I'd rather have a C average. It's my second year in this stupid class. I failed last year and I *have* to pass this year. I couldn't live through another year of this.

Counselor: Have you ever had a C in math for any quarter or grading period last year or this year?

Janet: Yeah.

Counselor: When?

Janet: Second quarter. It's been D's and F's since then. Mostly F's.

Counselor: The second quarter of *this* year?

Janet: Yeah.

Counselor: Just a couple of months ago?

Janet: Yeah.

Counselor: Wow. What was different about that second quarter when you got the C?

Janet: I just sat there and did my work, but now there's people around me talking and messing around and all that. And he blames it on me and kicks me out, but he doesn't kick them out. He'll give them a couple minutes after class and that's as far as it goes.

Counselor: Do you feel like he's picking on you?

Janet: Yeah.

Counselor: Singling you out and just trying to nail you?

Janet: Yeah.

Counselor: Okay.

Janet: He calls my home, too, and tells my stepdad stuff. Then my stepdad yells at me and I try to tell him it wasn't my fault. He says, "I don't want to hear it" and then I get grounded.

Counselor: So this math class thing is causing you some hassles at school *and* home.

Janet: Yeah. It's a real bite.

Counselor: Sounds like it. What are some things you've already tried to help improve your grades and get you to your goal of passing the class?

Janet: Asking more questions.

Counselor: What do you mean?

Janet: Sometimes I'll ask questions. I'll ask him how to do something and he'll say, "Put your hand down. Wait until later." Then he wonders why we don't turn in our work.

Counselor: So asking questions hasn't worked?

Janet: No.

Counselor: Okay. What other things have you tried?

Janet: I've tried sitting in the back and not saying anything.

Counselor: How did that work?

Janet: What do you mean?

Counselor: Did you get kicked out more or less when you sat in the back, compared to when you sat other places?

Janet: Less.

Counselor: So it worked out better for you?

Janet: It worked out better for me cause I was further away from him.

Counselor: Were your grades better or worse when you sat in the back?

Janet: Probably better, because I paid more attention and I took the work home to do. Plus, when I'm in the back, I'm not around my friends and that probably helps. My friends get pretty rowdy sometimes.

Counselor: Okay. Is it possible for you to sit in the back now?

Janet: I don't know. I guess. He doesn't care where we sit.

The Rest of the Story

During the remainder of the interview, the counselor and Janet discussed how she could do more of the things that had helped her get better grades, such as sitting in the back of the room away from her rowdy friends. Several specific strategies for improving grades were developed, and Janet implemented most of them. Disciplinary referrals decreased by about 50 percent following the counseling session. Although she did not reach her goal of earning a C in math, she improved enough to pass the course and to move on to the next year.

CASE DISCUSSION: "DROPPING THE ROPE"

Adults frequently engage in tug-of-wars with students in which the harder we try to change them or get them to see things our way, the harder they dig in and resist. When counselors, parents, or teachers try to coerce students into different beliefs about a school problem, power struggles usually result and the problem gets worse. *The most effective way to avoid power struggles in counseling is to "drop the rope" and work with rather than against the student's position.* In Janet's case, the ever-present power struggles that accompanied previous solution attempts were avoided when the second counselor worked *with* Janet's opinions of the problem and the teacher instead of trying to change them. After all, you cannot have a tug-of-war if no one is pulling the other end of the rope.

SUMMARY AND CONCLUSION

Janet's case offers important hints about what works and does not work in counseling middle and high school students. Adults frequently challenge students' opinions and positions that appear irrational or unfounded from an adult perspective. Unfortunately, this well-intentioned and "logical" tactic simply does not work well with most adolescents. In fact, it usually backfires and makes matters worse. Instead of trying to sell other people's ideas or to force Janet into changing (which had not worked in the first place), the second counselor approached her as a knowledgeable collaborator and consultant for improving her math grade. Janet was not resistant during the session, and she accepted and implemented the interventions. After all, it is hard to resist your own ideas! The counselor's enlistment of "students as consultants" (Murphy, 1994a) is central to the approach of this book.

In addition to accommodating Janet's opinion about the problem and the teacher instead of trying to change it, the counselor helped her discover and apply strategies that were previously successful in earning higher grades. Janet supplied all the necessary material for intervention. The strategy of utilizing successes, behaviors, and attitudes that are already part of the student's repertoire is more practical and effective than trying to teach brand-new behaviors or to coerce students into different beliefs.

PRACTICE EXERCISES

1. Select a small group of middle and high school students, and ask their opinions about what works best in adults' efforts to help them. Have them brainstorm some "dos and don'ts" that they would recommend to counselors who work with middle and high school students.
2. In your next counseling session, enlist the student as consultant by asking his or her opinion about how things might be improved regarding the school problem. If he or she responds positively to this, consider how his or her responses could be incorporated into the counseling process.

What the Research Says About
What Works

*Too many therapists take their clients out to a psychotherapeutic dinner and tell
them what to order. I take them out to dinner and say, "You give your order."*

—Milton H. Erickson

Janet's case as described in Chapter 1 illustrates some of the practical advantages of solution-focused counseling in schools. This chapter describes its empirical foundations by reviewing pertinent research and literature in the following areas: (a) factors that enhance counseling outcomes; (b) brief therapy; (c) collaborative problem solving in schools; (d) cultural considerations; and (e) counseling adolescents. These sources combine to form a strong rationale for solution-focused counseling in middle and high schools.

Examples and excerpts from actual cases are provided throughout the chapter to connect research findings to real world applications in middle and high schools. What works best in resolving middle and high school problems? This pragmatic question drives the remainder of this chapter and the rest of the book.

FACTORS THAT ENHANCE COUNSELING OUTCOMES

This section describes the contribution of various factors to successful outcomes in psychotherapy and counseling. Figure 2.1 is based on data from three decades of research on "what works" in helping people change (Lambert, 1992). This figure encompasses a broad and diverse range of clients, problems, and counselors. Successful change occurs primarily as a result of four interrelated factors. These factors, and their percentage contribution to successful outcomes, are as follows:

- *Client factors* (40%): personal strengths, talents, resources, beliefs, social supports
- *Relationship factors* (30%): empathy, acceptance, warmth

Figure 2.1. Factors that enhance counseling outcomes.

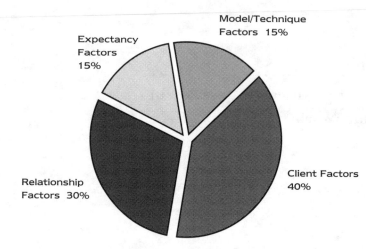

Note. Adapted with permission from Lambert, M. J. (1992). Implications of outcome research for psychotherapy integration. In J. C. Norcross & M. R. Goldfried (Eds.), *Handbook of psychotherapy integration* (pp. 94–129). New York: Basic Books.

- *Expectancy factors* (15%): hope and expectations for change
- *Model/technique factors* (15%): theoretical orientation and intervention techniques employed by the practitioner

These factors are interrelated in that the enhancement of one factor strengthens the others. For example, the effectiveness of a particular intervention strategy (model/technique factor) is enhanced when the student perceives the counselor as accepting and caring (relationship factor). Likewise, students, parents, and teachers become more optimistic (expectancy factor) when they are encouraged to apply their own strengths and resources to the problem (client factor).

Client Factors: The Filling

Factors of effective school counseling can be viewed as ingredients of a home-baked pie (Murphy & Duncan, 1997). Client factors represent the most important and essential ingredient in the pie, the filling. Attempting to change school problems without recognizing and encouraging the unique strengths and resources of students, parents, and teachers is like baking a pie without the filling. No matter what else you do, something is always lacking if the filling is missing or minimized.

Client factors are what students and others bring to counseling, including their unique strengths, beliefs, values, skills, experiences, ability to enlist the help and *support of others, potential for change and growth, and changes that are already happening.* Of all the factors that contribute to successful change in counseling, these are the most powerful (Garfield, 1994; Lambert, 1992).

The potency of client factors has important implications for the way we approach school problems and the people who experience them. Effective counseling helps people apply their own unique resources and skills toward resolving their difficulties (Lambert, 1992). In the case of Janet presented in Chapter 1, things improved when she was consulted about her own ideas and previous successes. Next, two client factors with important implications for middle and high school counseling are addressed: resilience and pretreatment change.

Resilience. The powerful role of client factors is evidenced in research on childhood and adolescent resilience. *Resilience* refers to a person's ability to successfully adapt or thrive despite adverse life circumstances and experiences (Garmezy, 1991). The notion of resilience is compatible with solution-focused counseling in its emphasis on what people do effectively and successfully in meeting life's challenges. Resilience research has consistently demonstrated that people are capable of remarkable accomplishments and changes when faced with problems. This research challenges pessimistic generalities about students from "disadvantaged" environments, and offers a source of encouragement for school practitioners who work with such students.

Studies of resilience have consistently indicated that client factors such as problem-solving skills and available social supports are correlated with successful outcomes (Rutter, 1985; Werner & Smith, 1982). Solution-focused counseling encourages students, parents, and teachers to recognize and apply such resources when dealing with school problems. For example, asking students how they have successfully handled other challenges in their lives may provide direction and ideas for approaching the current school problem. Research findings on resilience make a compelling case for identifying and utilizing people's strengths in addressing school problems, rather than focusing exclusively on their deficits and weaknesses.

Pretreatment Change. The empirical rationale for carefully attending to client factors is further strengthened by the discovery that desired changes may already be occurring before the student, parent, or teacher even walks into the counselor's office. *Pretreatment change* refers to desirable changes in the problem that are already in progress when the client enters counseling. In one study (Howard, Kopta, Krause, & Orlinsky, 1986), 15 percent of the clients indicated improvements in their problem situation prior to their first therapy session. Subsequent studies suggest that pretreatment changes may occur more often than this. In one study (Weiner-Davis, de Shazer, & Gingerich, 1987), 30 clients were asked if any positive changes occurred in the problem between the time they called for the appointment and their first session. Two-thirds of the clients reported that such changes had occurred.

When Lawson (1994) replicated this study using 82 clients, 60 percent reported positive changes.

Studies of pretreatment change support the first-session strategy of directly asking people if any positive changes in the problem have already begun. When students, parents, and teachers report pretreatment changes, counseling is simply a matter of encouraging more of what has already begun. Building on a pretreatment change is like tipping the first domino. One small change provides momentum for another, then another, and so forth.

Research on client factors encourages counselors to view people as resourceful and capable of improving their lives. These factors comprise the essential ingredient, or "filling," of successful counseling. Recognizing and utilizing client factors in addressing school problems is the heart of solution-focused counseling.

Relationship Factors: The Crust

Relationship factors are the second most important ingredient in the success of counseling. Returning to the pie metaphor, these factors serve as the crust or container of client, expectancy, and technique factors. *Relationship factors are those variables that are found in a variety of approaches regardless of the counselor's theoretical orientation, such as empathy, warmth, caring, genuineness, acceptance, and encouragement* (Carkhuff, 1971; Lambert, 1992; Rogers, 1951). In a comprehensive review of literature on the impact and components of effective helping relationships, Patterson (1984) states that "there are few things . . . for which the evidence is so strong as that supporting the necessity, if not sufficiency, of . . . accurate empathy, respect or warmth, and therapeutic genuineness" (p. 437). Orlinsky, Grawe, and Parks (1994) reviewed over 1,000 outcome studies and concluded that the quality of client participation in the counseling process was a strong determinant of outcome. Success is enhanced when people are included in the counseling process in an active, respectful manner.

The client's perception of the relationship strongly influences counseling outcomes (Gurman, 1977; Horowitz, Marmar, Weiss, DeWitt, & Rosenbaum, 1984). As suggested in Box 2.1, it is useful to ask people about their perceptions of counseling and the counseling relationship. Collaboration between practitioners and clients in determining the goals and focus of counseling is a major contributor to successful outcomes (Marmar, Horowitz, Weiss, & Marziali, 1986). In other words, counseling works best when the counselor explores content and goals that are relevant to the client.

Research on relationship factors suggests that counseling is more effective when students, teachers, and parents (a) experience the relationship positively, and (b) believe that the counselor is addressing what they see as important regardless of what others, including the counselor, deem to be

---

Box 2.1. When In Doubt, Ask the Client

Although researchers have developed some elaborate ways to assess people's perceptions of the counseling relationship, the easiest way to do this in everyday practice is simply to ask them. Consider the following exchange with Thomas, a 16-year-old student referred to the counselor for talking out in class.

Counselor: This is our second meeting, and before jumping in with things this week, I want to ask about our first meeting and how it worked for you. I want to know what I did that was helpful to you, or not so helpful.

Thomas: I think it went pretty well, but sometimes you asked me two questions before I had time to answer the first one. I thought it was cool that you asked me what I thought about things instead of telling me what to do. I had a counselor like that before. He was always telling me what to do like I was a little kid. That's not cool.

Thomas was very candid about his reactions to current and previous counseling experiences, which is not the case with every student. Even when students or others do not respond to such inquiries, the questions themselves imply our interest in *their* opinions and judgments.

---

important. As illustrated in the following case, *solution-focused counseling enlists powerful client and relationship factors by following the "3-A rule" of accepting, acknowledging, and accommodating the goals and beliefs of the client.*

Case Example: Clean More, Fight Less. A 10th grader named Susan complained of constant fighting with her father, stating that these conflicts were affecting her school work. This case illustrates the importance of client and relationship factors in promoting change. The following excerpt picks up during the first few minutes of the first interview with Susan.

Susan: I just started living with my father 2 months ago, and we're trying to learn to live together.

Counselor: That's quite an adjustment.

Susan: He's a bachelor and he has his ways. I've always lived with my mom. My father and I have two different opinions and we fight a lot.

Counselor: Can you give me an example of a fight?

[*The counselor accepts and accommodates Susan's language ("a fight"), which is intended to show empathy with her experience of the situation.*]

Susan described a "typical fight" as follows: (1) Susan asks her father's permission to go out with friends or to stay out later at night; (2) her father says no; (3) they argue; and (4) Susan leaves the room "in a huff" (slams the door, threatens to move out). Susan's goals were to fight less, go out more often, and stay out later. The fights prevented her from going out as often as she wanted. Susan believed that her father would allow her to go out more often, and to stay out later, if they fought less. Therefore, a change in the fighting situation was targeted as the primary goal.

Counselor: Tell me about the times you've been successful in going out without fighting with your father, or fighting less than usual.
[Asking about small successes and nonproblem times helps to shift the focus from what's wrong with clients to what's working for them. Focusing on a person's success and competency capitalizes on client and relationship factors by conveying the counselor's respect for the client's contribution to change. This type of question also invites clients to notice that the problem is not constantly happening, and to consider what they are already doing, if only just a little, to improve things. As evidenced in the next excerpt, Susan's response to the question initiates a solution cycle in which one idea leads to another, then another, and so forth.]
Susan: Sometimes it's better if I go over to a friend's house and call from there. He usually isn't in the mood for fighting over the phone because he doesn't want them to hear us.
Counselor: So that works pretty well for you?
Susan: Yes.
Counselor: Is there any way you can do that in the future?
Susan: Not every time. Sometimes he won't even let me go over to my friend's house, so I can't call.
Counselor: So you could do that sometimes but not all the time.
Susan: I guess. Or sometimes, if he's gone, I just leave a note and say that I'm going out.
Counselor: How does that work?
Susan: Okay, until I get back home.
Counselor: Is the fight when you get back home after leaving a note worse, better, or about the same?
Susan: It's better. It's not as bad.
Counselor: It's not as bad?
Susan: No.
Counselor: So, it's better when you use the phone before asking to go out, and when you write a note?
Susan: Yes.
Counselor: What else have you tried that seems to work well?
Susan: Cleaning something before I go.
Counselor: Like what?

Susan: Doing the dishes or straightening a room so I can say, "Well, I did this for you, so you should let me go." [*smiles*]
Counselor: That's a great idea.

During the remainder of the meeting, Susan and the counselor discussed how she could do more of the things that were already working toward her goals. Susan's goals and opinions regarding the problem were accepted, acknowledged, and accommodated. Susan commented that she had no idea she was doing anything that was helping, and added that "there might be some hope for us after all." As discussed next, hope is another key factor in the success of counseling.

Expectancy Factors: The Anticipation

Expectancy factors also contribute to successful outcomes, although their contribution of 15 percent is relatively smaller than that of client or relationship factors. In terms of the pie, expectancy factors refer to the anticipation and positive expectations associated with eating it. *Expectancy factors include clients' expectations regarding change, and their perception of the counselor's credibility.* A client's positive expectancy or "hope" regarding change improves counseling outcomes (Frank & Frank, 1991; Snyder, Irving, & Anderson, 1991).

The power of hope and expectancy has important implications in working with school problems. By the time teachers and parents request a counselor's help, they often feel demoralized and defeated by the problem, as do many students. Expectancy factors are enhanced when counselors emphasize possibilities for a better future without denying a person's pain and frustration regarding the problem. School practitioners can help people gain a sense of hope by (a) acknowledging problems *and* possibilities; (b) focusing on the future instead of the past; (c) believing in the competencies and resources of students, parents, and teachers; and (d) believing in the potential of the counseling process itself (Kottler, 1991).

Model/Technique Factors: The Topping

Model/technique factors refer to the particular theory or model adopted by the practitioner, and the intervention techniques based on that model. I used to think model and technique were the key factors of success. Find the right theory and technique, and the rest is all down hill. This is definitely not the case according to outcome research, which suggests that model/technique factors account for only 15 percent of the change occurring in counseling.

Outcome research indicates that a counselor's failure to attend to important client and relationship factors undermines the effectiveness of *any* intervention model or technique. As illustrated in Box 2.2 and in the following

---

Box 2.2. Rearranging Furniture Without Permission

Outcome research suggests that attempting to talk people into different beliefs is like walking into someone's house and re-arranging the furniture without their permission. As soon as you leave the house, most people move everything right back where they had it. Adolescents have taught me much in this regard. When I try to sell them *my* ideas, I can practically see these ideas dropping off of them as they walk out of the office.

---

case, one of the surest ways to paralyze an intervention is to impose it on a client against his or her will.

Case Example: The Making of an Impotent Technique. Sandra, a 10th-grade student, was referred by her mother (Rita) because of declining grades, poor study habits, and a "belligerent attitude." Rita and Sandra described their relationship as stormy and confrontational, especially when it came to school matters. Rita was a high school teacher, and good grades were very important to her. Sandra claimed that Rita was always "playing teacher" and telling her how to study. Rita tearfully stated that she was merely trying to help Sandra by sharing effective study strategies.

Rita was an intelligent and conscientious parent who had given her daughter's school problems a great deal of thought. Her suggestions for improving Sandra's study habits were worthy of a textbook. However, the harder she tried to get her daughter to implement these suggestions, the more resistant and belligerent Sandra became. Rita was very frustrated by Sandra's refusal to do the very things that would help her improve her grades in school.

As effective as Rita's study suggestions appeared to be, they were doomed to fail because they were unacceptable to Sandra. Sandra wanted to improve her grades, but was unwilling to accept any suggestions from her mother. One of the surest ways to "dis-empower" a good idea or technique is to force it on a student who disagrees with it, or who is not asking for help in the first place. Models and techniques are effective to the extent that they are accepted by the client; they become impotent when forced on unwilling recipients.

Returning to the pie metaphor, model/technique factors are like the pie's meringue or topping. Although important to the overall appearance and taste of the pie, meringue does not stand well on its own. Without the support of the filling and crust, the meringue falls flat. Models and techniques have very little influence on counseling outcomes when they are separated from client and relationship factors. In the solution-focused approach, the counselor's interpretations and techniques are selected on the basis of their compatibility with the client's beliefs and opinions. The client's acceptance of a theory or technique is a major determinant of its effectiveness, no matter how correct or appropriate the practitioner believes it to be. The following section addresses a body of research that offers additional encouragement and direction to school practitioners.

BRIEF THERAPY

Time is a precious resource for school practitioners. Any approach to school counseling must be practical and efficient if it is to be used at all. Can time-limited counseling be effective in resolving school problems? Research on brief therapy supports an emphatic "yes" to this question.

Time-limited counseling is supported by a large body of research indicating no reliable differences in effectiveness between long-term and short-term individual therapy (Budman & Gurman, 1988; Koss & Butcher, 1986; Koss & Shiang, 1994; Luborsky, Singer, & Luborsky, 1975; Orlinsky & Howard, 1986). Studies on the effectiveness of single-session therapy have also been encouraging (Hoyt, Rosenbaum, & Talmon, 1992; Talmon, 1990). In one investigation (Talmon, 1990), 88 percent of single-session clients reported that improvements in the problem had been maintained at 3- and 12-month follow-ups.

Garfield's (1994) extensive research on client variables offers some important clues as to why brief therapy works. First, most people seek help to resolve a specific, current problem rather than to gain insight, overhaul their personalities, or explore the past. Second, the majority of people who enter counseling expect that only a few sessions will be required. These findings are relevant to school practitioners in that most school counseling referrals involve a specific concern or complaint about a student by a teacher or parent, such as low grades or behavior problems, and a desire for rapid change. The effectiveness of time-limited approaches such as solution-focused counseling may be due in part to the practitioner's respectful accommodation of the client's goals and expectations, and willingness to structure the counseling process accordingly.

Most middle and high school counselors are responsible for scheduling and other administrative tasks, leaving little time for actual counseling. Counselors need approaches that are efficient and relatively easy to implement. Research findings on brief therapy challenge the popular belief that the longer the treatment, the better the cure (Budman & Gurman, 1988; Koss & Shiang, 1994), and support the optimistic notion that every contact with students, parents, and teachers is an opportunity for change (Hoyt et al., 1992; Talmon, 1990). These findings collectively provide a source of hope and encouragement for school counselors who may have only one or two opportunities to meet with people concerning a school problem.

COLLABORATIVE PROBLEM SOLVING IN SCHOOLS

In their discussion of collaborative problem solving in schools, Gutkin and Curtis (1990) emphasize the importance of a co-equal relationship between service providers and those with whom they work. The practitioner's role as a collaborator or facilitator is typically more effective in problem solving than an authoritative role (Greenberg, Elliott, & Lietaer, 1994; Reinking, Livesay, & Kohl, 1978; Updyke, Melton, & Medway, 1981).

Collaborative relationships are particularly useful in working with middle and high school students. The advantages of collaborating and negotiating with adolescents, instead of attempting to force them into compliance, have been noted by many researchers and clinicians who specialize in counseling adolescents (Brigham, 1989; Forgatch & Patterson, 1989; Selekman, 1993; Wexler, 1991). Teenagers sometimes perceive adults' efforts to help them as power plays designed to usurp their independence or coerce them into compliance (Brigham, 1989). Wexler (1991) states, "When adolescents feel forced into something, they resist. On the other hand, when they feel that they are choosing to do something for their own self-interest, their motivation can be intense" (p. 94).

Treatment Acceptability

Research on treatment acceptability strongly supports a collaborative approach to counseling. Treatment acceptability refers to the degree to which clients accept and agree with an intervention model or technique (Kazdin, 1980). Not surprisingly, interventions that are rated by parents and teachers as more acceptable are implemented more often than interventions rated as less acceptable (Elliott, Witt, Galvin, & Peterson, 1984; Reimers, Wacker, Cooper, & DeRaad, 1992). Witt and Elliott (1985) astutely point out that "a treatment that is not used is no treatment at all" (p. 253), regardless of how good it looks to the practitioner or on paper. As illustrated in Box 2.3, respecting and utilizing the client's own ideas about the problem and its potential solution is the surest way to promote acceptable interventions.

Empowerment

The notion of collaboration is closely related to the concept of empowerment in schools. In discussing empowerment, Dunst and Trivette (1987) offer the following recommendations for school personnel in their work with parents and students: (a) Offer suggestions in a way that fits with the individual's or family's own culture, and with their own appraisal of the problem; (b) promote the family's use of natural support networks and neither replace nor supplant them with professional services; (c) convey a sense of cooperation and joint responsibility for solving problems; and (d) help the family members not only see that the problem has been solved, but also that they functioned as active, significant change agents in the problem-solving process.

> **Box 2.3. Placing the Client's Opinions Above Our Own**
>
> Family therapist Jay Haley once commented that it was easy to think of various ideas for resolving a problem, but getting clients to do them was an entirely different matter. The greatest technique in the world is useless unless it is used. Based on the research in this chapter, the most effective way to increase the acceptability and implementation of an intervention is to recognize and utilize *the client's* ideas and resources in developing it. Problem solving is enhanced by placing the client's beliefs above our own theories and opinions regarding the problem and its solution.

Solution-focused counseling is compatible with the philosophy and techniques of empowerment. However, I do not believe that counselors can "empower" students, parents, or teachers by giving them something that they did not have prior to counseling. A solution-focused perspective maintains that people already have the resources and strengths necessary to improve their situation, and that effective counseling helps them discover and apply these resources to the problem at hand. Collaboration, empowerment, and respect for people's unique resources and strengths is further addressed in the following discussion of cultural considerations.

CULTURAL CONSIDERATIONS AND SOLUTION-FOCUSED COUNSELING

Recognizing that each person creates a different model of the world enables us to cherish rather than judge or fear those differences.

—B.A. Lewis and F. Pucelik, *Magic Demystified*

It is essential to consider the cultural responsiveness and inclusiveness of any school counseling approach in light of the growing diversity among the student population. The term *culture* is used in this book to encompass everything that defines a person and his or her world view, including ethnicity, gender, age, sexual identification, language, value system, and experiential background.

In discussing culturally and ethnically responsive counseling, Ridley (1995) advocates that counselors adopt a collaborative versus authoritative role in setting goals with clients. According to Ridley, a collaborative approach strengthens minority clients' sense of empowerment and ownership in the counseling process. Ridley asserts that "every client should be understood from his or her unique frame of reference" (p. 82), and that "clients are experts on themselves and capable of determining what goals serve their own best interests" (p.104). These statements accurately describe the respectful, accommodative nature of solution-focused counseling.

A counselor can effectively accommodate the client's views without "personally" agreeing with or ascribing to such views. Differences between the values and world views of clients and counselors are inevitable. Instead of attempting to impose a different cultural system onto clients, practitioners can explicitly accept and work within the client's culture. *The purpose of solution-focused counseling is to help people change school problems, not to convert them to the counselor's or anyone else's world view and culture.*

Vargas and Koss-Chioino (1992) highlight the importance of "building on pre-existing adaptive strengths" (p. 309) of ethnically diverse children and adolescents. Solution-focused counseling strongly emphasizes the discovery and utilization of students', parents', and teachers' strengths and resources in the process of resolving school problems. Respecting and accommodating what clients bring to counseling, that is, their culture and resources, is central to the solution-focused approach and to current recommendations and perspectives on multicultural (Goldenberg & Goldenberg, 1994; Ridley, 1995) and gender-sensitive (Brooks, 1992; Worell & Remer, 1992) counseling.

In this approach, the counseling process is adapted to clients instead of expecting clients to adapt to the counseling process. This accommodative theme is extended in the following discussion of unique considerations in counseling adolescents.

COUNSELING ADOLESCENTS

People are generally better persuaded by the reasons which they have themselves discovered than by those which have come into the minds of others.

—Blaise Pascal

The above quote from Pascal applies to people of all ages. However, its wisdom is perhaps most apparent in the context of counseling adolescents. The following discussion integrates professional literature and research on adolescence into some unique considerations for working with middle and high school students.

Developmental Considerations

This section presents an overview of adolescent development, with an emphasis on the relevance of developmental considerations in solution-focused counseling with middle and high school students. Adolescence is one of the most dramatic stages of human development. The following discussion highlights typical features of adolescence, along with the ages that are commonly associated with them. These features are presented as guidelines in understanding and counseling adolescents, not as predictions or prescriptions about individual students. There is considerable variation in the rate and nature in which these features are manifested among adolescents.

Early Adolescence (Middle School). Early adolescence usually refers to the ages of 11 through 14, although it may begin a bit earlier for girls and later for boys (Schave & Schave, 1989). These ages roughly correspond to the middle school years, grades 6 through 8, for most students. The transition from childhood to adolescence is characterized by dramatic physical, social, and psychological changes. Although these three domains of adolescent development are discussed separately below, they are highly interrelated. Changes in one area of development influence other areas. For example, noticeable changes in the body (physical domain) can significantly alter an adolescent's self-image (psychological domain).

Physical. Physical development in early adolescence is characterized by:

- increased muscular strength and control
- dramatic growth spurts in weight and height
- increased production of sex hormones and the onset of sexual maturity

As puberty begins and the physical maturity process unfolds during early adolescence, some students become "painfully aware of being more or less mature than their peers, developing 'locker room phobia,' because they do not want peers to see their bodies" (Vernon, 1993, p. 120). Rapid growth spurts and hormonal changes may also detract from the student's physical coordination and attractiveness during this period. These aspects of physical development are useful to consider in working with middle school students, parents, and teachers.

Social. Social development during the early adolescent period typically includes the following:

- separation from adult caregivers
- acquisition of new heroes
- stronger affiliations and attachments with peers

Social changes in early adolescence have important counseling implications. For example, a counselor's knowledge of a student's heroes may be useful in developing a cooperative relationship and designing interventions that are compatible with the people and things that are viewed as important by the student. Counselors can also help prevent or resolve problems by sharing information about social development with parents and teachers. For instance, parents may feel angry and hurt when their child begins to question their authority or to spend less time with them and more time with peers. A counselor's empathic explanation that their child is displaying a normal developmental transition can greatly assist the parents in understanding and coping with these changes.

Psychological. Psychological development of early adolescence includes:

- increased abstract thinking and ability to detect inconsistencies in logic
- heightened sensitivity to the moods of others
- recognition of the distinction between real and ideal
- increased mood swings and negative emotional states (apathy, shame, guilt, depression)

These changes can impact counseling in numerous ways. Middle school students are often vigilant and critical of perceived discrepancies between "saying" and "doing" on the part of parents, teachers, political figures, and other adults. Perceived discrepancies between the words and actions of adults may lead to some cynicism and disillusionment. Some adolescents become very disappointed and discouraged upon realizing that their real world falls far short of their ideal world. As middle school students develop a keener sense of other people's moods, they may exaggerate the significance of a teacher's, parent's, or friend's reaction to them or to something they have done. Adolescence is also characterized by more frequent and dramatic mood swings, which prompts some students to think they are "going crazy" (Newman & Newman, 1991). A basic knowledge of these psychological features helps counselors effectively relate to adolescents. For students who interpret their mood swings as a sign of "losing it," counselors can normalize their experience by explaining that mood swings increase during this age period and are not a sign of craziness.

Midadolescence (High School). Midadolescence generally corresponds to grades 9 through 12 and ages 15 through 18. Many of the developmental changes of early adolescence are extended and refined during midadolescence. This period also presents new challenges and changes for high school students.

Physical. Physical development during midadolescence generally involves a continuation or completion of early adolescent pubertal changes. Most females will achieve full breast growth during this period, and their body weight will generally become more evenly distributed (Newman & Newman, 1991). Males usually acquire more facial hair and their voice becomes progressively deeper. These physical changes can affect psychological and social development by influencing the way adolescents see themselves (psychological) and are seen by others (social).

Social. Peers continue to take on progressively more importance throughout midadolescence. Whereas early adolescent friendships are often linked to common activities such as sports, high school friendships are more likely to be based on abstract, higher-level factors such as shared beliefs and compatibility (Dusek, 1991). As a result, friendships generally become more enduring and stable than they were during early adolescence. Serious dating and sexual relationships may also occur during this period. As adolescents become more aware of sexual feelings, they develop stronger gender identifications. For those in the sexual minority such as gay and lesbian students, this period can be extremely difficult and marked by confusion, anger, and peer rejection (Colemen & Remafedi, 1989). It is helpful for high school practitioners to consider how these aspects of social development may influence specific school-related problems.

Psychological. The instability of early adolescence is gradually replaced by more enduring, stable patterns of thoughts, feelings, and actions. However, the gradual journey to stability may be marked by varying degrees of experimentation with different roles and behaviors. For example, experimentation with sexual relationships and drug use increase during this period (Carlson & Lewis, 1993). As students move through high school, they are progressively faced with important decisions regarding future schooling, career paths, and related options. This is both exciting and stressful for many adolescents. The exhilaration of new opportunities and freedoms is often coupled with a sense of isolation and vulnerability ("What if I make the wrong choice?"). Adolescents "face leaving the world that they have always known and stepping out on their own" (Wallbridge & Osachuk, 1995, p. 208). Increased privileges, such as driving a car and scheduling one's own time, also represent increased responsibilities. Freedom and responsibility represent two sides of a developmental coin that can become a major source of conflict between high school students and their caregivers.

Of all the issues in early and midadolescence, the establishment of independence and identity is perhaps the most important one for counselors to bear in mind while working with middle and high school students (Brigham, 1989; Wexler, 1991). The following section addresses the adolescent's quest for independence, with emphasis on the implications for solution-focused counseling in middle and high schools.

The Quest for Independence

Identity formation, individuation, and emancipation are considered to be major developmental tasks of adolescence (Bigner, 1994; Erikson, 1968; Havighurst, 1970). In the process of developing an identity separate from parents and others, adolescents may go to great lengths to develop and preserve their unique beliefs and values. Middle and high school students are very aware and suspicious of perceived infringements on their freedom to think for themselves. As illustrated in the case of Janet in Chapter 1, efforts to directly persuade or coerce adolescents out of their opinion and into an opposing viewpoint are usually counterproductive (Brigham, 1989). In discussing the importance of connecting with what the adolescent views as important, Wexler (1991) advocates that counselors try "to appeal to the inherent adolescent drive toward 'making life easier'," observing that "attempts at convincing teenagers that certain behaviors (aggression, substance abuse, or running away) are not 'right' elicit either immediate oppositional behavior or superficial compliance" (p. 37).

Students are often referred for counseling by teachers or parents. Therefore, they may not acknowledge that there is a problem at all, or they may view the problem as belonging to someone else. The story in Box 2.4 illustrates the futility of trying to sell our beliefs and ideas to clients who are not interested in buying.

An effective alternative to engaging in ideological tug-of-wars with adolescents is to accept and work within *their* beliefs and goals. Encouraging different behaviors in ways that are consistent with the student's goal ("getting parents or teachers off my case") is more effective than working toward goals that are stated in the words of others ("becoming more mature and responsible"). As illustrated in the next case example, honoring the input and preferences of adolescents paves the way for positive changes in school problems.

Case Example: When "Not Knowing" Is Smarter Than Knowing. Several years ago, a high school student taught me a valuable lesson about requesting the client's input before offering any suggestions of my own. Patti was referred for counseling by her teachers because of absenteeism and declining grades during the first half of her senior year. Patti's file referred to a prior sexual abuse experience in which she was molested by her father. Although our counseling goal was to improve grades and school attendance, Patti's comments regarding sexual abuse are highlighted in the following excerpt from our first meeting.

Patti: So are you some kind of expert on sexual abuse?
Counselor: No, I'm not an expert. Why do you ask?
Patti: I saw that book on your shelf.
Counselor: I see. I have read some things on sexual abuse, but most of what I've learned has come from people like you who have told me about their own experiences and reactions to it. Does that make any sense?
Patti: Yes. The last psychiatrist I went to babbled on about this and that. Repressed memory, masked depression [*laughs*]. I'm pretty smart with words, but half the time I didn't know what he was talking about.
Counselor: You mean talking about the sexual abuse?
Patti: Yes.
Counselor: Did you *want* to talk to him about it?
Patti: Yes. But *I* wanted to talk about it instead of hearing him droning on. He acted like he could read my mind. He would tell me how I felt and what I thought. Give me a break.

Box 2.4. George, the Dead Guy: Convincing the Unconvincible

George was referred to a psychiatrist by his wife because he thought he was dead. True to form, George entered the psychiatrist's office and boldly proclaimed that he was dead. The psychiatrist skillfully presented several rational arguments to convince him otherwise, none of which worked to change George's position. The psychiatrist became frustrated and said "Sir, you seem like a decent fellow. Why don't we talk about what's *really* bothering you and drop this stuff about being dead. What do you say, George?" George was touched by the doctor's concern, but steadfastly maintained that he was dead. Suddenly a brilliant idea occurred to the psychiatrist, and the following dialogue ensued.

Psychiatrist: George, are you absolutely sure you are dead?
George: Yes.
Psychiatrist: Would you be willing to participate in a scientific experiment to put your belief to the test?
George: Sure.
Psychiatrist: Tell me, George, do dead men bleed?
George: Of course not.
Psychiatrist: Would you allow me to gently prick your finger with a pin to see whether or not you bleed?
George: Sure.
[With that, the doctor pricked George's finger, which promptly began to bleed. George looked dejected as he stared at his bleeding finger.]
Psychiatrist: You can't escape the facts now, George. You have to admit you were wrong, don't you?
George: *[turning to leave the office]* Yes, doctor. I was wrong all along. Dead men *do* bleed.

[This story was adapted from *Friedman's Fables* (Friedman, 1990)]

Counselor: Well, I promise I can't read your mind, or anybody else's for that matter.
Patti: [*laughs*] Thank God.

I met with Patti four times throughout the remainder of the school year. Based on her comments regarding her previous counseling experiences, I listened a lot more than I talked during these sessions. I occasionally asked Patti what I was doing or not doing that was helping or hindering our work together, and she told me. She accomplished her counseling goal of passing all of her classes and graduating from high school.

Patti's comments during our last meeting of the year left a lasting impression on me regarding the importance of respecting the student's point of view.

Patti: Thank you for helping so much this year.
Counselor: You're welcome. What did I do that helped you the most?
Patti: You listened instead of telling me what to do. Nobody ever listens, but everybody has ideas about what to do, and they're not afraid to tell me. Do this, do that. It's like everybody is an expert on me except me. You didn't do that. You treated me like an adult instead of a weak little kid.

The recommendation to "never argue with the client," attributed to John Weakland of the Mental Research Institute, is particularly relevant to counseling adolescents. It is doubtful that Patti would have accepted any theories regarding sexual abuse until her opinions were respected and acknowledged.

Outcome research indicates that successful change is enhanced by the counselor's understanding and acceptance of the client's beliefs and opinions. One of the most common sources of conflict between adolescents and their parents or teachers is the adolescent's sense of being "misunderstood." Knowledge of adolescent development can improve a counselor's ability to empathize with some of the attitudes and actions of middle and high school students.

SUMMARY AND CONCLUSIONS

The empirical literature in this chapter supports a cooperative, solution-focused approach to counseling in middle and high schools. The following key points were described and illustrated.

1. Client factors such as unique strengths, talents, and resources represent the most powerful ingredients in successful counseling outcomes. Trying to change school problems by focusing exclusively on the deficiencies of students is like trying to bake a pie without the filling. Effective relationships and outcomes are enhanced when counselors accept, acknowledge, and accommodate the client's goals, beliefs, and resources. Counseling models and techniques are successful to the extent that they fit the unique characteristics and circumstances of clients.

2. Big problems do not necessarily require big solutions. Meaningful changes in school problems can occur in a short period of time. Every contact with a student, parent, or teacher is an opportunity for change.

3. Relating to students and others in a collaborative manner promotes their ownership, acceptability, and implementation of interventions.

4. Culture-sensitive counseling is enhanced by respecting and accommodating the client's unique beliefs, preferences, strengths, and resources (i.e., by fitting counseling to the client instead of fitting the client to counseling).

5. Adolescence is a period of dramatic physical, social, and psychological change. A counselor's knowledge of key developmental features of adolescence, such as the movement toward autonomy and self-direction, enhances effectiveness in working with middle and high school problems. Solution-focused counseling is very responsive to the adolescent quest for identity and independence.

PRACTICE EXERCISES

1. Outcome research indicates that the counselor's recognition and utilization of client factors improves counseling outcomes. Think of some ways that you have effectively utilized client factors such as successes, talents, and social supports. Think of some other ways you could capitalize on these factors in your work with students, parents, and teachers. Pick one of these ways and try it out in an upcoming counseling session.

2. Think of a student you are currently working with who is viewed as not having much to offer to the process of change and counseling. Take a few minutes to list some client factors associated with the student that might be useful in improving the problem for which he or she was referred. How might you incorporate one or more of these factors into the counseling process?

3. What are some things that you already do to instill hope in the students, parents, and teachers with whom you work? What are some additional ways that you could encourage hope in your clients?

3

Therapeutic Influences and Assumptions

I n addition to the empirical influences discussed in Chapter 2, the approach in this book has been strongly influenced by the following three sources: (1) the work of Milton Erickson; (2) the brief strategic therapy model of the Mental Research Institute (MRI); and (3) the solution-focused therapy model of the Brief Family Therapy Center (BFTC). This chapter describes and illustrates the major contributions of each of these approaches. The chapter concludes with six working assumptions of solution-focused counseling in middle and high schools.

THE WORK OF MILTON ERICKSON

Therapy is often a matter of tipping the first domino.

—Milton H. Erickson, in Rossi, *The Collected Papers of Milton Erickson*

The pioneering ideas and techniques of psychiatrist Milton H. Erickson, regarded by many as the founder of brief therapy, have had a major impact on the development of solution-focused counseling. Although Erickson developed his therapy approach prior to 1960, his work continues to be studied by therapists and counselors throughout the world. Of Erickson's many and varied contributions to the task of helping people change, the following elements of his work are especially relevant to middle and high school counseling.

No General Client, No General Theory

Erickson held no particular theory of psychopathology. When asked about his theoretical orientation or "general theory" of treatment, Erickson said that he did not have one because he had never met a "general client." He adapted his treatment approach to the unique characteristics and style of each individual client, instead of attempting to fit the client into some general theory or treatment approach. He viewed psychoanalysis and other psychological theories as fascinating and intriguing, but of little practical use in helping people change.

Time Effectiveness

Erickson was very "economical" in his approach to therapy (Haley, 1973). He demonstrated that meaningful therapeutic changes can occur quickly, and that effective therapy does not necessarily require the therapist's lengthy excavations into the origins and history of the problem. He spent relatively little time on the problem, focusing instead on the solution. Erickson was continually alert to change opportunities and possibilities. This practical, time-effective approach to counseling is encouraging to busy school professionals who have very little time to devote to each individual case.

Focus on the Future

Erickson's "pseudo-orientation in time" or "crystal ball" technique (Erickson, 1954) is a hypnotic intervention in which clients are directed to imagine a problem-free future, then to describe how they resolved their problem. This strategy taps the inner resources of people, and shifts their focus from the problematic past to a better future. Clients often report ideas and actions that fit their unique personalities, beliefs, and circumstances. According to Erickson, sometimes this is all that is required for solutions to emerge. The pseudo-orientation in time technique is the basis of the "miracle question" (de Shazer, 1985), a key strategy of solution-focused counseling.

Emphasis on Small Change

Erickson remained very alert to small changes in the direction of the client's goals. In describing Erickson's work, Haley (1973) states that "he seeks a small change and enlarges upon it. If the change is in a crucial area, what appears small can change the whole system. Sometimes he uses the analogy of a hole in a dam; it does not take a very large hole to lead to a change in the structure of the whole dam" (p. 35).

Utilization

Erickson's utilization of "whatever clients bring" to counseling is perhaps the most renowned aspect of his work. He viewed people as having a wealth of inner resources and competencies, and therapists as facilitators in helping clients recognize and apply these resources to the problem. According to Erickson, effective therapy is a process of expanding solution possibilities for clients instead of narrowing down treatment to the one and only "right" intervention. Erickson viewed clients who were experiencing problems as "stuck" versus "sick," and often utilized their hobbies, interests, and strengths in designing therapeutic interventions.

Prior to suggesting interventions to clients, Erickson carefully attended to (a) the language they used to describe themselves and their problem,

(b) their unique beliefs and values, (c) their strengths and resources, and (d) their nonverbal behaviors. He tailored his language and interventions to the client instead of expecting the client to conform to his language, beliefs, and theories. Accommodating the counseling process to the client is a central theme of this book.

Case Example of Erickson's Approach: The Student Who Refused to Read. Erickson's cooperative, efficient approach is demonstrated in the following case example involving a 12-year-old student named Paul. This case is described in Haley (1973).

Paul, a middle school student, was referred to Erickson because he was not reading. When given a first-grade reader, Paul typically would stumble through it, if he attempted it at all. His parents insisted that he could read, and deprived him of various privileges for several weeks in an attempt to get him to read. Despite the loss of privileges and other punitive measures, he still did not read.

Upon meeting with Paul alone the first time, Erickson expressed the view that Paul's parents appeared very stubborn in not accepting that he could not read. Erickson told Paul to "forget about reading" and to think of a fun way for them to spend the therapy hour. As Erickson questioned him about his hobbies and interests, Paul said that he enjoyed fishing, and that he hoped to go fishing with his father during the upcoming summer. Paul told Erickson that his father typically went fishing in California and Washington, but that he was planning a fishing trip to Alaska in the upcoming year. Erickson pulled out a map and asked for Paul's help in locating the specific towns in which his father fished. As Erickson confused certain towns on the map, Paul corrected him. They spent the next couple sessions "looking at" (*not* "reading") maps, discussing fishing techniques, and "looking up" different kinds of fish in the encyclopedia.

Observing Paul's sense of adventure and mischief, Erickson suggested that he play a joke on his teachers and parents the next time they observed him attempting to read. Erickson suggested that Paul take the first-grade reader and stumble through it just like he usually did, but that he do a little better on the second-grade reader, better yet on the third-grade reader, and so on. Paul thought it was a great idea, implemented it, and displayed no additional reading problems in the future.

In this case, Erickson effectively demonstrated the 3 A's of solution-focused counseling in middle and high schools: acceptance, acknowledgment, and accommodation. Erickson immediately accepted and acknowledged Paul's reading predicament. He accommodated Paul's interests, and his choice not to read, throughout the counseling process. Additional cases and descriptions of Erickson's work can be found in Haley (1985), O'Hanlon and Wilk (1987), and Rossi (1980).

THE MENTAL RESEARCH INSTITUTE

We find that in deliberate intervention into human problems the most pragmatic approach is not to question why? but what?; that is, what is being done here and now that serves to perpetuate the problem, and what can be done here and now to effect a change.

—P. Watzlawick, J. Weakland, and R. Fisch, *Change*

Influenced by the work of Erickson and convinced that meaningful therapeutic change can occur rapidly, a group of clinicians and researchers initiated the brief therapy project at the Mental Research Institute (MRI) in Palo Alto, California (Fisch, Weakland, & Segal, 1982; Watzlawick, Weakland, & Fisch, 1974). Over the years, many pioneers in the field of family therapy and psychotherapy have been associated with the MRI, including Gregory Bateson, Virginia Satir, Jay Haley, Steve de Shazer, John Weakland, and Paul Watzlawick, to name a few.

The Problem Process

The MRI brief therapy project involved a wide variety of clients and problems ranging from children to the elderly, and from schizophrenia to parent-adolescent conflict. As they studied more and more cases, the team noticed a consistent pattern in the way that most problems were developed and maintained (Watzlawick et al., 1974). This pattern is described below and graphically illustrated in Figure 3.1.

1. An ordinary life difficulty occurs, such as a difficulty at school, or feelings of sadness (Example: a seventh-grade student does not complete a couple of math homework assignments one week).
2. Attempted solutions are applied to the difficulty (Example: Parents lecture their child at length about the importance of timely homework completion; the math teacher reminds the student about homework each day at the end of class).
3. Solution attempts are unsuccessful, the difficulty persists or escalates, and "more of the same" solutions are applied (Example: The student misses two more assignments during the next week, followed by more lectures and reminders).
4. The difficulty comes to be viewed as "a problem," and solutions are applied even more vigorously, based on the belief that they represent the only sensible thing to do in response to the problem. In essence, "the solution becomes the problem" (Example: The student continues to miss homework assignments, and the teacher and parents continue to "lecture and remind").

Figure 3.1. The MRI problem process.

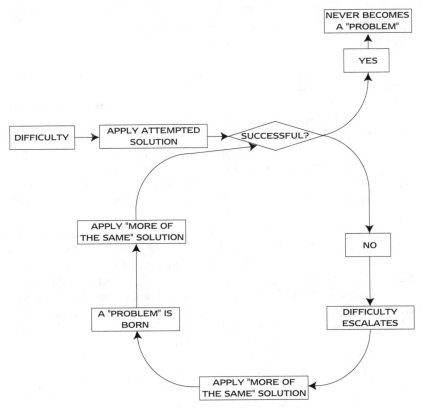

5. This problem cycle continues until someone "does something different."

The 9-Dot Problem in Appendix B illustrates how easy it is to get stuck in a pattern of "more of the same" solution attempts. The notion that attempted solutions can become part of the problem is an important consideration for school practitioners. One of the more common problem-solution patterns involving adolescents is the "responsibility trap." This occurs when well-intentioned adults, usually parents, attempt to resolve a school problem by taking on more and more responsibility for the problem while the student assumes less and less (Durrant, 1995). This pattern may persist for weeks or even months despite no major change in the problem.

Interrupting Ineffective Solutions

When solutions that are attempted by students and others become part of the problem, counseling seeks to interrupt ineffective solutions and to encourage people to respond in ways that are contrary to these solutions. MRI-based interventions are aimed at interrupting problem patterns by altering people's actions and perceptions associated with the problem.

Client Position

A counselor's suggestions to a client are more likely to be implemented if they are made with careful attention to the client's position regarding the problem (Fisch et al., 1982). "Position" consists of two main dimensions. *The first dimension of client position consists of the client's beliefs, opinions, and theories about the problem and its potential solution.* For example, teachers who view a student's classroom behavior as "manipulative" would be more likely to implement an intervention presented with a compatible rationale, such as "to regain control of your classroom," than they would if the same intervention was presented with a rationale that did not adequately fit their position, such as "to support and nurture" the child.

The second aspect of client position refers to the client's "customership" for change. Customership can be described as the nature and level of a person's commitment to change the problem. The person's customership strongly influences the type of interventions and suggestions that will be accepted and implemented. Fisch et al. (1982) developed some customership categories that were further elaborated by de Shazer (1988). The three categories are listed below. Fisch et al. (1982) and de Shazer (1988) emphasize the importance of acknowledging customership without viewing any one category as somehow "better" than the others.

Visitors. Visitors are not very interested in seeing things change or in doing anything about the problem. For example, students who are referred for counseling by teachers or parents may enter counseling as visitors.

Complainants. Complainants acknowledge that there is a problem, yet are unwilling to take any major action to resolve it. For instance, a teacher might readily acknowledge that a student's classroom behavior is a serious problem, yet may not be very willing to implement a classroom intervention to change the problem.

Customers. Customers acknowledge the problem *and* want to do something about it. For example, parents of a student referred for truancy may be very willing to try anything to improve their child's school attendance.

Consideration of client position is very helpful in deciding *what* to say to people and *how* to say it. The MRI emphasis on respecting and utilizing client position is one of the major reasons that this model has been so effective with "resistant" clients (Hayes & Melancon, 1989).

Case Example of the MRI Approach: Tripping the Responsibility Trap. The following case illustrates several aspects of the MRI approach. Note how the parents' position is accommodated in offering a suggestion intended to interrupt their existing solution attempts and to promote a different response to the problem.

Jerry was a bright and creative sixth grader referred by his parents and teacher for low grades. The low grades resulted mainly from minimal homework completion. Jerry's parents were hard-working, conscientious people who were willing to do anything to help their only son. The major theme of parents' solution attempts had been to plead, coax, and otherwise attempt to verbally persuade Jerry to complete his homework. This strategy remained in effect for the first 2 months of the school year. In addition to its ineffectiveness in improving things, this evening routine was very upsetting to both Jerry and his parents. The parents viewed Jerry as troubled, and saw the problem as an indication of his difficulty in adjusting to middle school. They expressed concerns about his irresponsible attitude toward school work.

A new and different homework routine was suggested to the parents, based on the rationale that their daily lectures and pleas regarding homework might be interfering with Jerry's opportunity to take personal responsibility for his school work. This rationale was intended to accommodate the parents' desire to help and support Jerry in school, and their concerns regarding his lack of responsibility for school work. They were advised to go about their usual business at home without lecturing or even mentioning homework. The parents accepted and implemented this suggestion. They reported rapid and significant improvements in Jerry's homework completion, adding that they had successfully applied this strategy to other areas of parenting.

By the time students are referred for counseling at the middle and high school level, many of them have heard the same old song from various adults and they can "smell it from a mile away." When adolescents express an unenthusiastic "been there, done that" response to our suggestions or ideas about the problem, it is best to try something different. The pragmatic wisdom of the MRI is captured in the second of two simple guidelines of solution-focused counseling: *If it doesn't work, do something different.* The first guideline, *if it works, do more of it,* evolved primarily from the efforts of another innovative group of clinicians addressed next.

THE BRIEF FAMILY THERAPY CENTER

Historically psychotherapy has concerned itself with problems (variously defined) and solutions (seldom defined at all), with the problems receiving the major share of the effort. In fact, solutions have been looked at so rarely that solution has become the hidden half of the "problem/solution" distinction.

—Steve de Shazer, *Clues*

The term "solution-focused therapy" was coined in the 1980s by Steve de Shazer and colleagues at the Brief Family Therapy Center (BFTC) in Milwaukee, Wisconsin (de Shazer, 1985; de Shazer et al., 1986). The team at the BFTC extended Erickson's work by focusing on (a) the future versus the past,

(b) solutions versus problems, and (c) clients' strengths versus deficiencies. Unencumbered by a specific theoretical orientation, the BFTC pragmatically sought to identify what works in helping clients change. They routinely videotaped and analyzed therapy sessions for this purpose. The remainder of this section describes some of the observations and discoveries of the BFTC that are particularly relevant to school counseling.

Skeleton Keys

One of the most fascinating observations of the BFTC was that certain interventions were effective for most clients, regardless of the specific nature of their problem. These strategies were viewed as "skeleton keys" that could fit any type of problem (de Shazer, 1985). The BFTC team concluded that the counselor does not have to know a lot about the problem in order to help the client resolve it. They also found that problems were resolved much quicker when therapists and clients focused on solution-related details and possibilities rather than focusing on problem history, presumed causes, and other problem-related details.

Using the skeleton key metaphor, the BFTC shifted their focus from the intricacies and details of the lock (the problem) to the possibilities of the key (the solution). If one's main purpose is to help clients open the door to solutions, it is highly inefficient to spend a lot of time studying each lock. It is more productive to simply insert the keys into each lock, which is exactly what the BFTC team and their clients began to do with the problems they encountered.

The Formula First Session Task

One of the first skeleton keys or "formula interventions" developed at the BFTC became known as the formula first session task (FFST). The FFST was presented to clients at the end of the first session in the following way:

Between now and the next time we meet, I would like you to observe, so you can describe to me next time, what happens in your [pick one: family, life, marriage, relationship], that you want to continue to have happen. (de Shazer, 1985, p. 137)

The FFST is broadly applicable to many types of problems, including school problems. Clients frequently return to the second session with additional ideas and hope regarding solutions to the problem. They are encouraged to focus on, and do more of, whatever they want to see continue happening in their lives. As the BFTC team focused more and more on future solutions instead of past problems, they discovered two other useful avenues of change—the "miracle question" and "exceptions."

The Miracle Question

The miracle question, based on Erickson's crystal ball technique, is a unique way of orienting people to a better future and promoting a positive expectancy of change. In the miracle question, the client is asked:

> Suppose that one night, while you were asleep, there was a miracle and this problem was solved. How would you know? What would be different? (de Shazer, 1988, p. 5)

Most people enjoy contemplating this question, and it helps them to define more precisely what they want from counseling. For example, a parent or teacher who wants the student to become more independent and responsible might respond to the miracle question by adding concrete details such as "bringing the car home on time" and "completing schoolwork with less reminders from me." In addition to shifting the client's focus from the problem to the solution, these concrete signs of improvement serve as criteria for evaluating the effectiveness of counseling.

Exceptions

One common element of the FFST and the miracle question is the emphasis on times and circumstances in which the problem does not occur, referred to as "exceptions" to the problem (de Shazer, 1988). In addition to these two formula interventions, the BFTC developed other ways of discovering and utilizing exceptions, including direct questions such as, "Tell me about times during the last week when the problem occurred less often or not at all." Encouraging people to identify exceptions helps them focus on what to do instead of what not to do in order to resolve the problem.

Keeping It Simple

Another contribution of the BFTC that is particularly well suited to the practical realities of school counseling is the notion of keeping it simple. The BFTC team observed that sometimes all you need is a small change in the way someone perceives or acts upon a problem to initiate its solution. The practical notion of starting small and keeping it simple is captured by the question, "Why use a bazooka when all you need is a squirt gun?" In solution-focused counseling, practitioners are encouraged to start with small, simple interventions for school problems before attempting strategies that are more involved and time-consuming.

Case Example of the BFTC Approach: Growing Solutions From the Small Seeds of Success. This case illustrates the importance of keeping it simple and utilizing exceptions to the problem. The parents of an 11th-grade student (Tonia) requested that I meet with their daughter. Their concerns centered on the increasing conflicts between Tonia and her mother which had escalated in recent weeks. Most of the arguments occurred shortly after Tonia arrived home from school.

Early in our first meeting, I explored exceptions to the problem by asking Tonia if there were any times in which she and her mother were able to talk without fighting. After quickly answering "no," Tonia corrected herself and recalled that they did not fight at all when they talked about flowers and gardening, a hobby they both enjoyed. We discovered some other common interests and topics that the two of them might be able to talk about without fighting. We playfully referred to these topics as DDTs ("Do-able Discussion Topics"). An experiment was suggested in which Tonia would (1) initiate a conversation with her mother about flowers or another DDT every day after school, and (2) observe how well they got along for the rest of the day. Tonia returned the next week and reported that she and her mother still argued about things, but not nearly as frequently or intensely as they had the week before. No additional concerns were reported that year by Tonia or her parents.

The highly pragmatic, straightfoward approach of the BFTC is well suited to the practical realities of counseling in middle and high schools. As illustrated throughout this book, a solution orientation toward what is working for the student and others is applicable to a wide variety of problems and situations encountered by school practitioners. This orientation drives the central guideline of solution-focused counseling: *If it works, do more of it.*

ASSUMPTIONS OF SOLUTION-FOCUSED COUNSELING IN MIDDLE AND HIGH SCHOOLS

The following assumptions are derived from research on what works as presented in Chapter 2, and from the therapeutic approaches of Erickson, the Mental Research Institute, and the Brief Family Therapy Center. These pragmatic assumptions guide the process of solution-focused counseling in middle and high schools.

ASSUMPTION #1: If It Works, Do More of It. If It Doesn't Work, Do Something Different

This assumption captures the straightforward and practical nature of solution-focused counseling. In regard to doing more of what works, this approach utilizes exceptions and other client resources in order to resolve school problems. When people's attempted solutions are contributing to the problem, solution-focused counseling draws on numerous strategies for interrupting ineffective solutions by changing the "doing" and "viewing" of the problem.

ASSUMPTION #2: Students, Parents, and Teachers Have the Necessary Strengths and Resources to Change School Problems

Based on research indicating the potency of client and relationship factors in the process of change, the success of counseling is enhanced when we relate to students, parents, and teachers as resourceful and capable. It is easy for students and others who are dealing with a school problem to become demoralized and lose sight of their strengths, competencies, and resources. In the midst of a serious problem, especially one that has occurred for a long time, people tend to develop a "problem-saturated" view of themselves and their circumstances (White & Epston, 1990). Solution-focused counseling encourages students, parents, and teachers to discover and apply their competencies and resources to the problem at hand.

Students, parents, and teachers experiencing a school problem are viewed as "stuck" versus "sick." Problems are seen as temporary roadblocks resulting from limited recognition of alternatives, not as symptoms of underlying pathology. Students are enlisted as valuable consultants and collaborators in the change process instead of being treated as passive players in an "adults only" version of school counseling. Viewing and responding to people in this way enhances their self-efficacy (Bandura, 1977), and creates solution opportunities that would otherwise be overlooked or minimized.

ASSUMPTION #3: A Small Change in Any Aspect of a School Problem Can Initiate a Solution

This assumption is based on the ecological notion that a small change in any aspect or element of a system can ripple into larger, more significant changes (Plas, 1986). Big problems do not necessarily require big solutions. This is particularly encouraging to school counselors who have neither the time nor the resources to engineer highly complex, time-consuming interventions for every school problem presented to them. The notion that small changes in any aspect of a problem situation can initiate solutions also provides flexibility and optimism in choosing what specific aspects of the situation to work on, and who to work with at any given point (parent, student, teacher, school administrator, etc.), given that changes in the perceptions or actions of anyone associated with the problem may help resolve it.

The ecological emphasis of solution-focused counseling does not deny the existence of intra-individual limitations such as neurological problems or academic skill delays. These factors can significantly influence school performance and should be dealt with accordingly. However, even in these situations, the approach's emphasis on small changes in the perceptions or social interactions surrounding the problem may complement other treatments such as medication or modified academic instruction.

ASSUMPTION #4: A Focus on Future Possibilities and Solutions Enhances Change

Solution-focused counseling focuses on the future instead of the past, and on solutions instead of problems. An emphasis on the future helps clients and counselors pursue solutions instead of avoiding problems. Effective counselors do not deny the pain and frustration experienced by people who are dealing with a serious school problem, nor do they ignore important details of the problem. People are invited, not forced, to focus on solutions of the future instead of problems of the past. Most people welcome this opportunity and find it to be a refreshing change.

ASSUMPTION #5: There Are Many Possible Meanings and Interpretations for Any Given Behavior. If One Particular View or Theory Is Not Working, Toss It and Try Another

In order to make sense of our experiences, we are constantly constructing meanings for the events and circumstances of our lives. These "personal constructs" (Kelly, 1955) influence the way we interpret and respond to our own behavior and the behavior of others. The exact same event or behavior can be viewed very differently by different people. Teacher A might view a student's rare participation in class discussions as a sign of laziness and apathy, whereas Teacher B interprets the student as respectful and quiet. Although neither view is better or more right than the other, one view may be more useful in promoting change in a particular school problem.

When we regard a particular view or interpretation as the one and only truth, problem-solving strategies may be limited to only those that fit this view. As Durrant (1995) states, "Beliefs about self and others keep people from noticing information . . . that would allow them to . . . move forward" (p. 12). Viewing a school problem from multiple perspectives allows us the flexibility to choose those perspectives and strategies that are most likely to promote change.

ASSUMPTION #6: Cooperation Enhances Change

Counseling research indicates that successful outcomes are more likely in the context of a cooperative counselor–client relationship. Cooperation is enhanced by respecting and accommodating the goals, opinions, and resources of students, parents, and teachers (Murphy, 1996). The notion of "constructed meanings" addressed in Assumption #5 provides counselors with the flexibility to select interpretations and interventions that fit clients and their unique circumstances.

SUMMARY AND CONCLUSIONS

1. The work of Milton Erickson highlights the importance of approaching each client and case as unique from all others, and tailoring our interac-

tions and suggestions accordingly. Erickson's time-effective focus on bringing about small changes in the problem fits well with the practical realities of school counselors.

2. The brief therapy model of the Mental Research Institute illustrates how people's well-intentioned solution attempts may perpetuate the very problem they are intended to resolve. In these cases, counselors encourage clients to do or view the problem differently. The MRI model also highlights the importance of utilizing client position throughout counseling.

3. The solution-focused therapy model of the Brief Family Therapy Center introduces the notion of "skeleton keys" or "formula interventions" that appear to work well with most people and most problems. The strategy of building on people's existing strengths and successes is an efficient, optimistic way to approach school problems. The BFTC model suggests that change occurs more rapidly when counselors and clients focus on future solutions rather than past problems.

4. The therapeutic wisdom of these approaches was integrated with the empirical research of Chapter 2 to formulate six working assumptions of solution-focused counseling in middle and high schools.

PRACTICE EXERCISES

1. Erickson effectively utilized clients' beliefs, attitudes, and skills to develop solutions to their problems. Pick a case during the upcoming week and think about how the student's unique beliefs and talents could be utilized to change the school problem.

2. Think of a current case in which people's attempts to resolve the problem appear to be making it worse. What could you suggest to the clients in this case to interrupt their ineffective solution attempts while respecting their beliefs and opinions regarding the problem?

3. During the next week, try out the Formula First Session Task (FFST) by asking one or two of your clients to make a list of the things in their lives that they want to continue happening. Ask them what they have done, and are currently doing, to make these things happen. For a more personalized experience of this task, make a similar list pertaining to you and your life. Ask yourself what you did to bring these things about, and what you can do in the future to sustain them. Observe differences in the way that you and your clients react to focusing on what works instead of what does not work.

Steps and Strategies of

Solution-Focused

Counseling

4

Cooperating for a Change: Establishing and Maintaining Effective Relationships

. . . clients usually only hear when they feel that they have been heard, when their experiences have been validated.

—B. Cade and W. H. O'Hanlon, *A Brief Guide to Brief Therapy*

Cooperation is the glue of solution-focused counseling—the unseen yet essential element that holds everything together. The effectiveness of any intervention strategy rests largely on the extent to which it is accepted and owned by the person expected to implement it. Cooperative relationships enhance the acceptability and ownership of interventions on the part of students, parents, and teachers.

This chapter presents guidelines and strategies for establishing and maintaining cooperative, change-focused relationships with clients. These guidelines are operable from the very first contact regarding the problem, and throughout the entire counseling process.

ADOPTING THE "AMBASSADOR" PERSPECTIVE

Tell me, I forget. Involve me, I understand.

—Ancient Chinese Proverb

One way for counselors to establish and maintain cooperative relationships is to approach students and others like an ambassador approaches a foreign country or culture (Hubble & Solovey, 1994). Effective ambassadors maintain an open mind in order to learn as much as possible about the people with whom they are visiting. They ask questions and listen carefully to the answers. They respect and accept diverse cultures and world views, even when such views differ markedly from their own. Successful ambassadors do not promote their own opinions, goals, and methods. Instead, they help people articulate and pursue goals that are important *to them*, employing and offering methods that are compatible with the opinions and resources of their clients. Ambassadors are continually alert to new understandings, alliances, and possibilities.

The collaborative or ambassador approach to counseling strongly contrasts with authoritative approaches in which counselors *tell* clients why the problem has occurred and what to do to about it, with minimal input from the client. The ambassador perspective can be conveyed to students and others by being curious and tentative instead of certain and absolute. Although this may seem like a strange position to adopt in working with students, consider how a middle or high school student might react to the following set of comments from a counselor. In both cases, the counselor's goal is to introduce the student to a different view of teachers.

Comment #1 (the "Absolute and Certain" Counselor): When we met last week, you were saying that your teachers were too strict and that they didn't care about you. I've thought about that, along with some other things we discussed, and I have to tell you that you've got your teachers all wrong [statement of certainty]. They actually care a lot about you. It is precisely because they care about you that they take the time and effort to make sure you do your homework and get good grades [the phrase, "it is precisely because," implies the absolute one and only truth]. Do you understand?

Comment #2 (the "Curious and Tentative" Counselor): When we met last week, you were saying that your teachers were too strict and they didn't care about you. I'm *wondering* if there could be any other *possible* explanations for what your teachers are doing [statement of curiosity]. *I'm not sure* if this is on target [tentative statement], but you're the best judge of that so I'll tell you what I was thinking and let you decide. *Could it be that* one of the reasons your teachers get on your case about turning in homework and getting good grades is because they *might* actually care enough about you to remind you to turn it in so you can get better grades? *I don't know,* what do you think?

Commentary on Comments #1 and #2: Attempting to coerce adolescents into different beliefs is a futile endeavor. One of the surest ways to reduce the effectiveness of a potentially useful idea or strategy is to try to force it on someone against his or her will, as the "absolute and certain" counselor did in Comment #1. Most people want to actively participate in resolving their problems. The counselor in Comment #1 disregards this notion and thereby jeopardizes the client–counselor relationship.

The counselor in Comment #2 offers the same alternative view of the teacher in a tentative manner that conveys a sense of curiosity and exploration. Given the typical adolescent's tendency to strive for independence and autonomy, a counselor's ideas and suggestions are more likely to be heard and accepted when they are presented in the tentative manner of Comment #2 as compared to the authoritative style of Comment #1. Presenting an idea as a possibility instead of a certainty is usually more effective in promoting change. If the student chooses to reject an idea, the counselor's credibility remains intact and other possibilities can then be considered. Fisch et al. (1982) recommend that counselors adopt a tentative position to increase their maneuverability and flexibility instead of boxing themselves into a corner by presenting their ideas as absolute truths and certainties.

Curiosity

The ambassador perspective is useful throughout the counseling process, even after positive changes in the school problem have occurred. Positive changes in the problem can be explored by the following types of questions:

- How did you manage to change things so quickly?
- What have you been doing differently to bring about these changes?
- I'm curious about how these improvements have occurred. Can you help me understand what's been happening to make things better?

The counselor's curiosity about how people made important changes in the problem helps them to reflect upon and clarify what they did to bring about such improvements. As Cade and O'Hanlon (1993) point out: "It is often much better to maintain a puzzled skepticism rather than a crusading zeal" (p. 98).

Confusion

The ambassador perspective can also be expressed by the practitioner's confusion. Some have likened this aspect of solution-focused counseling to the style of the fictional TV detective, Columbo (Selekman, 1993), as described in Box 4.1. Expressing confusion instead of certainty about a client's view is an effective, cooperative way to encourage them to consider other views.

Adopting the ambassador perspective is not some devious tactic used to trick students and others into changing. It is an honest and respectful way to approach people about whom counselors know very little, which includes most clients.

COOPERATING WITH CLIENT POSITION

Client position (Fisch et al., 1982) refers to a client's beliefs, opinions, and theories regarding a school problem and its solution, and to his or her motivation and commitment to resolve the problem (customership). Customership is a unique solution-focused concept that is unfamiliar to many school practitioners. The following section provides a more thorough discussion of customership, along with specific strategies for accommodating the customership of students, teachers, and parents.

Box 4.1. Columbo the Counselor

Television detective Frank Columbo routinely employed confusion strategies in order to gather important information about a crime and its solution. Like Columbo, middle and high school counselors can utilize confusion to promote changes in the way students view and act on school problems. Consider the following example: "You know, I think I'm missing something here. It wouldn't be the first time that happened. Anyway, help me out here. You were saying that the teachers don't care about you, but then you said that they get on your case about doing homework and getting good grades, right? Well, I'm confused. A lot of the teachers that I had in school who were pretty strict about homework and grades were the ones that seemed to care the most about me and the other students. I had some teachers that let us do anything we wanted, and it seemed like they were just in it to collect their paychecks. Can you help me understand this thing a little better?" Selekman (1993) notes that the Columbo approach is particularly useful in "engaging some of the toughest adolescent clients" (p. 103).

Customership

Chapter 3 introduced the customership categories of visitor, complainant, and customer to describe the manner in which a person approaches the counselor and the counseling process, including their motivation and commitment to resolve the problem. Determining a client's customership for change includes the following considerations:

- How important is this problem to the client?
- How willing is the client to do something about it?
- How inconvenienced or put out by the problem is the client?
- Does the client accept any ownership of the problem?

Customership is assessed by paying attention to *what* clients say and *how* they say it. In order to cooperate effectively with clients, it is equally important to carefully consider what we say and how we say it.

Customership has important implications for the style and content of conversations with students, parents, teachers, and others involved with a school problem. The following scheme of customership, and related implications for counselors, is adapted from Fisch et al. (1982), de Shazer (1988), and Berg (1991).

Visitors. A visitor typically comes to counseling because he or she is somehow forced into it by another person (such as a parent or teacher) or agency (such as juvenile court). Visitors may be uncommitted to changing the problem and may not even acknowledge that a problem exists. Because visitors typically enter counseling under duress, the counselor's suggestions and interventions are likely to remain just that—the *counselor's* suggestions. It is highly unlikely that a counselor's suggestions for changing the problem will be accepted and implemented by a person who approaches counseling as a visitor. Unfortunately, visitors are often labeled "resistant" or "uncooperative" when they do not implement a counselor's suggestion.

Most middle and high school students enter counseling under a parent's or teacher's direction, and may not be highly motivated to take action on a problem that is defined by someone else. Parents may also approach counseling as visitors if they have not experienced major problems with their child at home, or if their behavioral expectations for the child are very different from those of school personnel.

In support of the term *visitors* to describe these situations, de Shazer (1988) comments: "Simply thinking about the situation as 'visiting' may be more useful than the therapist's thinking she has 'involuntary clients' whom she has to convince that they really need therapy" (p. 87). The following guidelines are useful in responding to situations in which students or others present themselves as visitors.

1. Refrain from trying to make the visitor "do" something. This usually solidifies the visitor position even more and reduces the effectiveness of future suggestions and interventions.
2. Acknowledge the person's point of view ("I can see how lousy this is for you to have to come in here and meet with me"), and work within that view to promote a change ("What do you think needs to happen for you to not have to come here anymore?").
3. Compliment the visitor on his or her position and presence at the counseling session ("I am impressed that you have the courage to come in here to meet with me"; "It is refreshing to meet someone who listens more than they talk"; "I really appreciate your willingness to take time from work to come here and try to help your child in school").
4. Renegotiate the goal of counseling to make it more appealing and meaningful to the person ("Would you be interested in working on ways to get your teacher and parents to stop hassling you about school?").
5. Discuss topics unrelated to the school problem, such as hobbies and special interests. Exploring these topics not only helps maintain cooperative relationships, but may also reveal skills and interests in other areas of the person's life that might be applied to the school problem.

6. Include other people who are more willing to do something about the problem. For example, if the parents are not very concerned about a school problem, it is usually more effective for counselors to focus their attention and efforts on the student and teacher instead of trying to motivate the parents.

Complainants. A complainant is someone who acknowledges the school problem and is willing to talk about it, but unwilling to take action toward resolving it. Complainants may view themselves as innocent bystanders who are relatively powerless in influencing a change. Change is considered to be someone else's responsibility. For example, a teacher may believe that the primary responsibility for solving a student's problem lies with the parents.

The following suggestions are helpful in working with complainants regardless of whether they are students, parents, teachers, or others.

1. Listen and give compliments.
2. Refrain from making action-oriented suggestions.
3. Offer new questions, perspectives, explanations, or interpretations regarding the problem that might encourage different responses from the complainant. For example, to parents who maintain that it is solely the school's responsibility to improve their child's school behavior, the counselor might respond with the following question: "Given that you, as parents, know your child better than anybody else, what suggestions do you have for us in helping her at school?" This question acknowledges the parents' position while encouraging their involvement as "consultants" to school personnel. In addition to asking such questions, it is helpful to reframe the problem, that is, to offer different perspectives or explanations that may encourage complainants to respond differently to the problem ("I wonder if Melissa's boisterous classroom behavior is more of an attempt to make friends and impress others than to disrupt your class").
4. Ask complainants what they would do if they were the counselor, or what suggestions they would make to others who are more actively involved with the problem.
5. If tasks are given, they should not require big changes in the way the person acts on the problem or goes about his or her daily routine. It is often useful to give tasks that require complainants to "reflect upon," "observe," or "predict" something pertaining to the problem, with the rationale of helping the counselor and complainant learn more about the situation.

Reflection Task: "Since you know a lot more about this student and this situation than me, it would really help me if you could reflect on what you think might work in making things better. The things you come up with do not have to relate to your classroom or even to school. It is not necessary to do anything differently about the situation or the student, just to give it some thought."

Observation Task: "In order to help me get a better handle on the situation, I would appreciate it if you could observe the things this student does that contribute to her success in your class."

Prediction Task: "I wondered if you would be willing to make a prediction each morning on whether or not this student is going to have a good day or a bad day. Write your predictions down on paper, then calculate your percentage of hits and misses at the end of the week."

The connection between these tasks and solutions to school problems may appear to be somewhat remote. However, they represent effective ways to cooperate with complainants and to keep them engaged in counseling (de Shazer, 1988).

Customers. A customer approaches counseling with a definite desire to do something about the problem. Customers can be identified by statements like "I'll do anything you suggest," "I've tried about everything I know to change this," and "I was hoping you could give me some ideas and techniques." Customers are usually the people who are most inconvenienced by the problem and who express a sense of urgency regarding its solution. In middle and high schools, this is typically the teachers and parents. However, the customer category may include students as well. Counselors can effectively cooperate with customers in the following ways:

1. Suggest action-oriented tasks such as behavioral interventions and other strategies that actively involve the customer.
2. Explore and utilize the customers' ideas about the problem and potential solutions. Ask what they would do if they were the counselor, and what suggestions they might make to others who were dealing with this type of problem.
3. Keep the customer involved in the problem-solving process, and keep them informed about progress.

Table 4.1 describes each customership position, along with strategies for cooperating with these positions.

It is important to view these categories of customership as guidelines rather than static realities or descriptions of a person's overall character or personality. A client's customership position may change throughout the course of counseling. For example, a student who enters counseling as a visitor might become a customer when the counseling goal is stated in a way that is more relevant and appealing to the student.

It is also important to view each position from a neutral standpoint. Customers have traditionally been viewed as "good" or "ideal" clients, ready and willing to implement the practitioner's suggestions. In the solution-focused approach, however, one position is not viewed as any better than the others.

Table 4.1. Description and Accommodation of Customership Positions

Position	Description	Cooperative Strategies
Visitor	Does not perceive a problem, or views it as belonging to someone else Enters counseling under duress Referred to counseling by someone else (teacher, court) Uncommitted to changing the problem	Refrain from action-oriented suggestions Acknowledge their position and point of view Compliment them on positive aspects of their presence or position Renegotiate the problem and goal in a way that is more appealing and meaningful to them Discuss nonschool topics, such as hobbies and interests
Complainant	Acknowledges the problem and its significance, yet may be unwilling to do much about it Views self as "innocent bystander" who is relatively powerless to change the problem Views responsibility for problem solving as belonging to others	Refrain from action-oriented suggestions Listen and give compliments Offer new questions and perspectives ("reframe") Enlist as problem-solving consultant and brainstorm potential solutions Assign reflection, observation, and prediction tasks
Customer	Acknowledges the problem and its significance, and is willing to take action to resolve it Desires active involvement in problem solving	Suggest action-oriented tasks Explore and utilize their ideas on the problem and potential solutions Communicate regularly about progress, and otherwise keep them actively involved in the problem-solving process

USING THE LANGUAGE OF COOPERATION AND CHANGE

Counseling sessions are linguistic exchanges between counselors and clients. Our conversations with students, parents, and teachers influence the way they respond to school problems. The language of counselors and clients can be an asset or a liability to the goal of changing school problems. Solution-focused counseling utilizes the power of language to enhance cooperation and promote change. The remainder of this chapter describes and illustrates two of the most potent therapeutic uses of language: (1) matching the client's language and position, and (2) using presuppositional language.

Matching the Client's Language and Position

Understanding implies that you can "join" a person at his own model of the world. This is important because people tend to operate as if their model of the world is the real world.

—B. A. Lewis and F. Pucelik, *Magic Demystified*

In addition to monitoring one's own language in relating to students and others, careful attention to *what* clients say and *how* they say it is crucial to effective counseling. Matching the language and position of students, parents, and teachers helps to (a) establish rapport, (b) validate their experience and opinions, (c) promote a cooperative working relationship, and (d) increase the likelihood that interventions will be accepted and implemented. Each of these elements enhances change in counseling (Lambert, 1992; Marmar et al., 1986; Patterson, 1989). Although the strategies of matching people's language and position overlap in actual practice, they are addressed separately for the sake of clarity.

Matching the Client's Language. The words and phrases that people use to describe a school problem provide important clues to the meanings and beliefs they attach to the problem. These clues provide direction for counselors in maintaining cooperative relationships and suggesting interventions that fit client beliefs. Although matching the client's language is important in dealing with people of all ages, it is especially so in working with adolescents.

Matching the language of middle and high school students does not require that counselors try to be ultracool by using all the latest adolescent lingo and expressions. This tactic usually backfires because it is perceived by most students as phony and insincere. On the other hand, the use of certain key words or phrases indicates the counselor's acceptance of the student's perspective. Although matching the client's language is important in working with teachers and parents, the following section focuses primarily on matching the language of students, because this is usually more of a challenge than matching another adult's language. Two brief examples, *how not to* and *how to*, are used to illustrate the importance of observing and matching the language of middle and high school students.

Example #1: "How Not To" Match the Client's Language. Instead of matching the student's language, the counselor in the following illustration tries to sell the student a different set of words to describe the problem.

Counselor: Why do you think Mr. Riehle [eighth-grade science teacher] referred you to me?

Eighth-Grade Student: He's a jerk, that's why. He *gets on me* all the time. He has it out for me. He lectures all the time about stupid stuff, and then he wonders why we flip out and screw around so much in class. Nobody likes him. He *gets on a lot of people.* He can't teach, so he yells at us instead. He ought to refer himself for counseling. I'm tired of him *getting on me all the time.*

Counselor: C'mon, now. That's pretty harsh, isn't it?

Student: What do you mean?

Counselor: Well, don't you really mean that he's firm and wants to run class in an organized way?

Student: What?

Counselor: It sounds to me like the two of you have a communication problem or a personality conflict.

Student: If you say so [*shrugs shoulders, pulls hat over forehead, scoots down in the chair, and is on the way to being labeled a "resistant" client*].

Example #2: "How To" Match the Client's Language. Observe the differences between the previous exchange and the following interview in which the counselor accepts and matches the student's language.

Counselor: Why do you think Mr. Riehle referred you to me?

Eighth-Grade Student: He's a jerk, that's why. He *gets on me* all the time. He has it out for me. He lectures all the time about stupid stuff, and then he wonders why we flip out and screw around so much in class. Nobody likes him. He *gets on a lot of people.* He can't teach, so he yells at us instead. He ought to refer himself for counseling. I'm tired of him *getting on me all the time.*

Counselor: How does he *get on you?*

Student: He's always asking me questions that he knows I won't be able to answer. He sends me out of class to the principal's office for little stuff. There are some people in there that mess around a lot more than me and never get sent out.

Counselor: What else does he do that *gets on you?*

Student: He says bad stuff about me in front of the whole class. Instead of talking to me in the hallway, he does it in front of everybody else. I hate that.

Counselor: Have you found any things that you can do in class that make him *get on you less* or be *less of a jerk?*

Matching some of the key phrases in the student's language instead of challenging them assisted the second counselor in establishing a cooperative versus combative relationship. When adolescents' description of a problem is directly challenged or criticized by the counselor, they often become more combative or simply shut down in the counseling process. Matching the language of students is one of several ways for counselors to acknowledge and accommodate their perspectives of the problem and its solution.

Many middle and high school students who are considered difficult or rebellious will go to great lengths to defend their autonomy and beliefs. Some students will endure the loss of privileges at school or home, refuse to do school work that they are capable of doing, and even jeopardize their graduation from high school in order to make a point regarding their independence and freedom.

When counselors cooperate with students' beliefs instead of "pulling the other end of the rope" and challenging them, students often shift their energies from defending themselves to examining their behavior and choices in relation to their goals. As students begin to examine their situation more objectively, they typically become more motivated to resolve school problems.

Many so-called stubborn or reluctant teenagers decide to improve their school performance when they discover that the counselor is not going to challenge or criticize their beliefs. It is as if they suddenly realize, "Hey, now that I don't have to argue with anybody about this, I can stop and think about what I'm doing and whether or not it's getting me where I want to go." Change is enhanced when counselors cooperate with students in a way that helps them shift their focus and energies from defending their freedom to examining their choices and behavior in relation to their goals for school and life.

Matching the Client's Position. Matching the beliefs and opinions of students, parents, and teachers is another valuable strategy of solution-focused counseling. People are likely to cooperate with questions, ideas, and suggestions that are compatible with their position. Tailoring an intervention to the beliefs and preferences of clients does not require the counselor's personal agreement with such beliefs. It is simply a more practical and efficient way to promote change than trying to persuade people to abandon their positions (Conoley, Ivey, Conoley, Scheel, & Bishop, 1992).

Consider the following conversation between a counselor and teacher regarding a seventh-grade student named Carrie. In this example of "how not to" match the client's position, the counselor jeopardizes cooperation by challenging the teacher's position and trying to promote a different one.

Example #1: "How Not To" Match the Client's Position.

Teacher: Every time I tell Carrie to do something, she talks back or does something to let me know she doesn't like it. She can be very manipulative with me and the other students.

Counselor: Manipulative is a pretty harsh word. Could it be that she just wants more of your attention or more attention from the students?

Teacher: Have you ever seen her in class?

Counselor: Well, no, I haven't.

Teacher: Come in some time and see what you would call it. She openly defies my instruction and terrorizes other students. Yes, she needs attention alright, but the way she goes about getting it is by being defiant and mean. You really need to observe her in class to understand what I'm saying.

Counselor: Well, I just believe that terms like manipulative and defiant are not real helpful ways to view students because they set up a battle between the teacher and the student.

Teacher: But it *is* a battle. She's battling me for control of the class, and she's winning.

Counselor: I just don't think you're going to be real effective with her if you view this as a battle.

Teacher: Come into the classroom sometime and see what you would call it.

Criticizing or minimizing someone's position on a school problem is one of the surest ways to create an impasse in counseling. People quickly recognize when their beliefs are being challenged, and usually respond by digging in and defending their position even more strongly (see Box 4.2). Some people, like the teacher in this example, make it pretty clear that they do not appreciate or accept the counselor's criticism. Others may respond by shutting down and not saying much in order to avoid being criticized. This is the last thing a counselor wants to happen given the powerful role of client opinions and resources in the ultimate success of counseling (Lambert, 1992).

In the following example of "how to" match the client's position, the counselor accepts and matches the teacher's position instead of trying to change it.

Example #2: "How To" Match the Client's Position.

Teacher: Every time I tell Carrie to do something, she talks back or does something to let me know she doesn't like it. She can be very manipulative with me and the other students.

Box 4.2. What Was YOUR Reaction?

Think about an experience you have had in which your personal views and beliefs on an important subject, such as politics or religion, were challenged by someone who knew very little about you and the bases of your beliefs. What was your reaction? Did the challenge seem to weaken or strengthen your original beliefs? Most people solidify their position even more in response to such challenges, especially when the challenge comes from people who do not know them well. *Regardless of how insightful we believe ourselves to be as counselors, we can never know a person as well as they know themselves.*

Counselor: What does she do that is manipulative?

Teacher: I'll ask the class to do an assignment and sometimes she'll just say "I'm not doing it" right out loud so everybody can hear it. Or she'll make fun of other students when they answer a question. If she makes a mistake or something doesn't go her way, she tries to turn it around to make it seem like it's my fault. She openly defies my instruction and terrorizes other students. She can be real defiant and mean. It's like she's battling me for control of the class.

Counselor: Who's winning the battle?

Teacher: At this point, I'd say she is.

Counselor: It must be a huge challenge dealing with this day in and day out.

Teacher: Believe me, it is.

Counselor: A lot of people would have thrown the towel in after one or two weeks of this kind of stuff. How have you managed to hang in there?

Teacher: Good question. I don't know. I guess I consider it a personal challenge to not let her get the best of me. But I'm about at the end of my rope now. That's why I wanted to talk with you.

Counselor: Maybe we can come up with some things that might help you hang onto the rope and to gain more control. What kinds of things have you already tried with Carrie?

Using language that effectively matches the language and position of clients is a very practical way to cooperate with people in changing school problems. The next section describes another useful way to cooperate and promote change.

Using Presuppositional Language

Words are, of course, the most powerful drug.

—Rudyard Kipling

O'Hanlon and Weiner-Davis (1989) describe *presuppositions* as questions or comments that presume something without directly stating it. Trial lawyers use presuppositional language to subtly influence the jury's perception of a witness. Consider the following question from a prosecutor to a business executive accused of embezzlement: "Are you still stealing from the company?" Either way the question is answered, "yes" or "no," there is a presupposition that the witness had at one time embezzled money from the company.

In solution-focused counseling, presuppositional language is used to encourage positive expectations of change and to mobilize client resources. Consider the following examples of presuppositional questions for students, parents, and teachers. The italicized words convey the presuppositional aspect of each question.

- What *will* be different in school *when* you start attending class more often?
- How *will* you know *when* things get a little better between you and your daughter?
- Which one of your students *will* be most surprised by your change in classroom management strategies?

Like solution-focused counseling itself, presuppositions are future-oriented and competency-based. Presuppositional language conveys the counselor's faith in the likelihood of change and in people's ability to improve their lives. The following case illustrates the use of presuppositional language in interviewing a student.

Case Example: What If Things Were Better, Raul? Raul, an eighth grader referred by the school and court for truancy, met with the school counselor the day after his court appearance. The juvenile court judge recommended increased parental supervision, an evening curfew, and counseling for Raul. School disciplinary measures included calling Raul's parent when he was absent, after-school detention (which he usually skipped), and grade penalties. The following dialogue occurred early in the counselor's first meeting with Raul.

Counselor: I read all the stuff from the court report. There's a lot going on, huh?

Raul: Yeah.

Counselor: What would you like to see happen?

Raul: I want everybody to back off. They're making it seem like I'm a criminal or something. All I've done is skip school a few times. It's not like I murdered somebody.

Counselor: What will be different about your life when people start backing off?

Raul: What do you mean?

Counselor: How will your parents treat you differently when you start coming to school a little more?

Raul: I guess they won't ground me as much or talk to me all the time about skipping school.

Counselor: What else will be different when you come to school more often?

Raul: I just won't have to get all dressed up to go to court and stand there and listen to all this stuff about the trouble I'm in.

The presuppositional questions in this session laid the groundwork for exploring small changes that Raul was willing to make in order to be treated better at home and school. Although his school attendance did not improve dramatically, he began to attend school more regularly. The people at court and school backed off accordingly. These changes probably would not have occurred as rapidly, if at all, had the counselor followed suit with the exclusive problem focus of previous interventions. Presuppositions invite people to view their situation from a hopeful perspective, and to shift their thinking from the static qualities of the problem to the dynamic possibilities of its solution.

Table 4.2 outlines the various strategies for establishing and maintaining cooperative, change-focused relationships.

Table 4.2. Strategies for Establishing and Maintaining Cooperative, Change-Focused Relationships

Strategy	Description	Examples
Adopt the "ambassador" perspective	Be curious, confused, and tentative in presenting questions and ideas Request clients' help in understanding their views of the situation	"I'm wondering if there might be another explanation for your teacher's behavior" "I need your help in understanding how you managed to do so well on your science test"
Match the client's language	Use words and phrases that the client uses to describe the problem Incorporate the client's language into goals and interventions	"What could you do in social studies class to make your teacher *back off* and *get on you* less?" "I wonder if you would *get hassled* less if you would occasionally ask the teacher a question in class. What do you think?"
Match the client's position	Acknowledge and accommodate both aspects of position: (1) the client's beliefs, opinions, and "theories" regarding the problem and its solution (2) the client's customership for change	Make suggestions and comments that are compatible with the client's beliefs and opinions Structure counseling to fit the client's position of visitor, complainant, or customer (See Table 4.1)
Use presuppositional language	Include words and phrases that presuppose change and solution	"What *will* be different *when* you start going to class more?" "How *will* you know *when* things *start getting better?*"

SUMMARY AND CONCLUSIONS

This chapter provided the following guidelines for establishing and maintaining effective relationships with students, parents, and teachers:

1. Approach clients from the perspective of an ambassador requiring their help in clarifying the nature of the problem, their position, and their problem-solving resources and competencies.

2. Assess and accommodate the visitor, complainant, and customer positions from which clients approach the counseling relationship. Remember that these descriptions are pragmatic guidelines, not static realities or descriptions of a person's overall character or personality. A person's customership may change during the course of counseling.

3. Recognize the power of language. Match and fit your language to key phrases and themes of the client's language and position.

4. Use presuppositional questions and comments that convey a positive expectation for change and that invite clients to shift their focus from the problems of the past to the possibilities of the future.

PRACTICE EXERCISES

1. Select a problem and have your partner interview you from the ambassador perspective for about 5 minutes. Next, have your partner interview you from a more authoritative or expert perspective. Observe the differences in your reactions to these different interviewing strategies. Switch roles and interview your partner from these two perspectives.

2. Think of a recent situation in which you connected particularly well with a student, parent, or teacher. What did you do to make that happen? Which of these things could you do with other clients in other situations?

3. Practice the following interviewing strategies with a partner: (a) matching the client's language, (b) matching the client's position, and (c) using presuppositional language. Practice each strategy for about 5 minutes, then switch roles. Discuss some of the unique challenges of using these strategies with students, parents, and teachers.

4. Pick a case you are currently struggling with, and describe the counseling process through the eyes and experience of the client. What new ideas has this exercise given you in regard to this particular case and client? How can these ideas be applied toward establishing and maintaining an effective counseling relationship with the client?

Interviewing for Solutions

*Solutions to problems are frequently missed because they often look like mere
preliminaries; we end up searching for explanations believing that without
explanation a solution is irrational, not recognizing that the solution itself is its
own best explanation.*

—Steve de Shazer, *Clues*

The conversations we have with clients can strongly influence the way
they view themselves and the problem. Our initial contacts with students, parents, and teachers are particularly important in this regard.
This chapter describes the powerful role of interviewing in solution-
focused counseling, with emphasis on the first (and perhaps only) interview. Following a short comparison of traditional and solution-focused
interviewing, several specific questions and strategies are provided to help
counselors make the most of their interviews with students, teachers, and
parents.

COMPARISON OF TRADITIONAL AND
SOLUTION-FOCUSED INTERVIEWING

*We are continually faced by great opportunities brilliantly disguised as insoluble
problems.*

—Mark Twain

The following discussion highlights some key differences between traditional
and solution-focused interviewing.

Interventive Versus Diagnostic Interviewing

Most approaches break the helping process into two distinct phases, assessment and intervention. Interviewing is viewed as a one-way process in which

the practitioner asks questions in order to size up and diagnose the client and the problem. The goal of the traditional diagnostic interview is to assign a label or classification to the client. Classifications typically include information and speculations regarding problem history, presumed causes, and prognosis. Traditional interviewing is driven by the assumption that the more one knows about the problem, the more likely it will be resolved. From this perspective, treatment does not begin until *after* the problem and client have been diagnosed.

In contrast to the traditional distinction between assessment and treatment, this chapter presents interviewing as the first step of intervention. Because the solution-focused approach does not distinguish between interviewing and intervention, every contact with a student, parent, or teacher is an opportunity for change. A single interview question can initiate a solution by shifting the way a person views the problem. For example, simple questions such as, "How will your teachers and parents treat you differently when your grades get a little better in school?," and "What will be the first small sign that this student is becoming more responsible in your class?," can help people shift from a past-oriented focus on what is wrong to a future-directed focus on possibilities and change. Tomm (1987) coined the term *interventive interviewing* to convey the notion that the interview itself can be a powerful mechanism of change.

Search for Solutions Versus Pathology

Sarason (1982) has harshly criticized the "search for pathology" that dominates assessment and intervention with children and adolescents. The initial interview traditionally yields a "laundry list of all the things that are wrong with the client" (Berg, 1991, p. 9). This can result in both client and counselor becoming overwhelmed by the size of the problem (Berg, 1991). Furthermore, extensive information about what people do poorly, or not at all, may not provide a clear direction on how to help them change.

School counseling referrals typically emphasize what's wrong with students. Cumulative school files of difficult students are often inches thick and include extensive documentation of problems and shortcomings. Although such information might be helpful in understanding a school problem, an exclusive focus on what's wrong with a student may steer counselors into a pessimistic attitude about the possibility of change before counseling even begins. As illustrated in the following experience, the search for pathology usually results in finding it.

Case Example: Seeing What (and Who) You're Looking For. Several years ago I was asked to observe a fourth-grade student named Bobby, whose teacher was concerned about his autistic-like behaviors in class. As I entered the classroom, the teacher discreetly informed me that Bobby was wearing a white shirt and was sitting in the first row by the windows. The teacher explained a math assignment, arranged the students in groups of four, and instructed them to complete the assignment as a group. During my 10 minutes of observation, Bobby spent approximately 75 percent of the time looking out the window and twirling his pencil. I recognized both of these behaviors as characteristic of autistic children. Staring out the window was an indication of the "social avoidance" symptom, while pencil twirling fit the "repetitive, self-stimulatory hand movements" of many autistic children.

As I walked up to the teacher's desk to share the results of my observation, she said, "He didn't do anything for you, did he?" When I showed the teacher the data I collected, she informed me that I had been observing the wrong student! I had observed Scott, who sat in the same row as Bobby and was also wearing a white shirt. The teacher explained that Scott was an academically gifted student who daydreamed when he became bored with easy assignments.

In addition to teaching me to make sure I am watching the right student during classroom observations, this was a powerful lesson on the notion that *we often see what we're looking for.* As illustrated in this example and in Box 5.1, the popular phrase "seeing is believing" might just as accurately be stated as "believing is seeing."

Our choices about *what* to look for are strongly influenced by the assumptions we make about people and problems. *Solution- focused counseling expands the lens of assessment and interviewing from an exclusive focus on the problem and deficits to a focus on solutions and strengths.* The active search for solutions begins in the very first contact regarding a school problem based on the assumption that it is easier to increase existing successes and competencies, no matter how small, than it is to eliminate problems. Information about what people are already doing or capable of doing to resolve school problems is generally more useful than extensive information on problem history. O'Hanlon and Weiner-Davis (1989) point out that counselors frequently get

---

Box 5.1. Hammers and Nails

"When the only tool you have is a hammer, everything looks like a nail."

—Abraham Maslow

This phrase describes our natural tendency to see what we are looking for, a type of self-fulfilling prophecy. While not ignoring important information regarding the problem, solution-focused counselors expand the focus of interviewing by seeking out the client's competencies, resources, and successes.

stuck "because they have too much information rather than too little, or too much information about the problem and too little about the solution" (p. 38).

SOLUTION-FOCUSED INTERVIEWING STRATEGIES

There are many procedures and sources for gathering useful information about a school problem besides interviewing, including testing, rating scales, school records, and so forth. However, interviewing seems to be the most common and accessible method for counselors to explore school problems and solutions.

Initial interviews are aimed at promoting change by defining and clarifying the problem, solution attempts, client position, goals, exceptions, and other client resources. The extent to which each of these areas is explored varies from case to case, as does the order in which they are explored. Each area is pursued in a cooperative context in which the counselor adapts interview questions and comments to the client's unique beliefs, style, and circumstances.

The Problem

Solution-focused counseling does not routinely involve lengthy explorations of problem history or presumed causes unless people indicate a definite preference for this. However, some basic information about the problem is usually helpful.

Defining A Changeable Problem. A clear definition of the school problem for which help is being sought has been recognized as an important step toward resolving it (Bergan & Tombari, 1976). *A problem that is stated in clear, specific, behavioral terms is more changeable than a vaguely stated problem.* For example, it is easier to change the number of times a student starts conversations with peers, attends school, or completes a classroom assignment, than it is to change the student's depression, irresponsibility, or attention deficit disorder.

Our everyday language is full of vague descriptors and labels that mean different things to different people. Students, parents, and teachers often present complaints in vague and abstract ways, as well as including interpretations in their descriptions of the problem. A teacher might describe the situation as a "motivation problem." Without further clarification, the problem will remain largely unclear and unchangeable. Fisch et al. (1982) recommend gathering "information that is clear, explicit, and in behavioral terms—what specific individuals say and do in performing the problem, . . . rather than general statements or explanatory interpretations" (p. 69). O'Hanlon and Wilk (1987) similarly advocate *videotalk definitions* of the problem, as described in Box 5.2.

Box 5.2. Videotalk

The encouragement of "videotalk" (O'Hanlon & Wilk, 1987) is particularly useful when a student, teacher, or parent describes a school problem in terms that are vague ("attention problem") or interpretive ("disrespectful"). Useful, factual descriptions of a problem can be obtained by asking clients to describe the problem in videotalk as if they were narrating the play-by-play events and actions of a sporting event. Consider the following videotalk descriptions of a student's "attention problem":

- When I ask the class to line up for lunch, she usually just sits there until I remind her a second time.
- She never completes all the problems on the daily math sheet I hand out in class.
- She taps her feet on the floor and moves around a lot at her desk.

These divergent descriptions of an "attention problem" highlight the importance of obtaining clear, observable definitions of the problem from the client's perspective. The more concretely and specifically a problem is described, the easier it is to change. Each of the three problem definitions above are more clear and changeable than the vaguely stated "attention problem." Encouraging students, teachers, and parents to use videotalk is a practical way to obtain specific problem definitions.

The following questions and requests are useful in helping people define clear, changeable school problems:

- If I videotaped the problem, what would I see and hear?
- Describe a recent example of the problem.
- If I were a fly on the classroom wall, what would I see?
- Tell me what the problem looks like.

Clarifying Related Circumstances. Clarifying the circumstances and patterns surrounding a school problem may provide important clues for how to go about changing it.

When? Some school problems regularly occur at certain times of the day, week, month, or year. The following questions are useful in determining such patterns:

- Is the problem more evident in the morning or afternoon?
- Does the student do this more in some classes than others?

- Have things been better, worse, or about the same during the past week?/month?/quarter?

Where? The following questions clarify connections between the problem and specific settings:

- Does the problem usually occur in one particular place (classroom, lunchroom, hallway)?
- Does the problem occur more frequently when the student is seated in the front of the room as compared to the back?
- Are things any better or worse in one place as compared to another?
- Does the problem usually occur during or in between classes?

With Whom? School problems may vary in the presence of different people. The following questions can be used to explore this area:

- Who is usually around when the problem occurs?
- Which teachers report more/less of a problem?
- Does the problem occur more often with one particular teacher/parent?
- Does the problem change depending on who the student is with?

What Happens Right Before and After? Events that precede and follow the problem are important in understanding and altering it. The following questions are useful in exploring this aspect of the problem:

- What is usually happening right before the problem?
- What are the student and others saying and doing right before the problem happens?
- Is the problem more likely to occur during a certain type of instruction (group discussion, individual seatwork, small group activity)?
- What happens right after the problem? Then what?
- How does the teacher/parent usually respond to the problem?
- What do they say? What do they do?
- How do the other students respond to the problem?

Table 5.1 summarizes the task of clarifying the problem and related features, including the client's solution attempts and position.

Solution Attempts

Ineffective solution attempts may become an integral part of the problem (Watzlawick et al., 1974). For this reason, it is important to ask students, parents, and teachers the following types of questions:

- What have you done about this problem so far?
- How did it work?

Table 5.1. Clarifying the Problem and Related Features

Strategy	Description	Useful Questions
Define the problem	Obtain a specific, behavioral description of the problem	If I recorded the problem on a video camera, what would I see and hear? What does this student *do* that is "irresponsible?"
Clarify the circumstances surrounding the problem	Obtain a clear description of the pattern and context of the problem	When does this problem usually occur? Who is usually around? What happens right before the problem? What happens right after?
Clarify solution attempts	Obtain a clear description of attempts to resolve the problem, and their relative effectiveness	What have you done about the problem so far? How did it work? What have others suggested doing about it? Of all the things you've tried, which one worked the best?
Clarify client position	Assess the client's belief and customership regarding the problem and its solution	What do you think is causing the problem? What do you think might help improve things? How much of a problem is this for you on a scale of 1 to 10, where 1 is "no problem" and 10 is "a major problem?" How willing are you to do something about this problem?

- What have others done?
- What have other people suggested doing about it?

Information regarding how students and others have dealt with a problem, and the relative success or failure of such efforts, provides valuable information for intervention purposes. For example, information about what has not worked well helps counselors to avoid more of the same.

In the midst of dealing with a difficult and frustrating school problem, people sometimes forget what *has* worked successfully in dealing with the problem or similar problems. The following questions help people recall what has already worked well, or to consider different ways of dealing with the problem:

- Of all the things you tried, which strategy worked best, if only just a little better than the others?
- How have you handled similar situations in the past?
- What kinds of things have you thought about doing but have not actually done?
- What kinds of things might you or others try that would be really different than anything that has already been tried?

I have seen many students, parents, and teachers develop solutions for a school problem by reflecting on previous successes and doing more of what has already worked with the problem or with similar challenges. In addition to providing counselors with ideas about what to do and not to do in approaching a school problem, the exploration of solution attempts conveys respect for people's experience and opinions of the problem.

Client Position

Don't oppose forces; use them.

—R. Buckminster Fuller

Client position includes a person's (a) beliefs and opinions regarding the problem and its solution, and (b) customership for change. It is important to clarify people's position early in the counseling process by listening to *what* they say and *how* they say it.

Beliefs and Opinions. The following questions are useful in assessing an individual's beliefs, opinions, and theories regarding the problem and solution:

- What is your theory about this problem?
- What do you think is causing the problem?
- What do you think might help improve things?

Customership for Change. A person's customership for change can be assessed with the following types of questions:

- Of all the people involved with this problem, who seems most troubled by it?
- How is this problem affecting your life?
- How willing are you to do something about this problem?
- Of all the worrying being done about this problem, what percent of it are you doing? What percent is your teacher/parent doing?

Goals

A journey of a thousand miles begins with one step.

—Confucius

It is essential to establish a clear picture of what the solution looks like in the eyes of the client. Positive change in school problems is enhanced when practitioners "begin with the end in mind" by clarifying goals at the outset of counseling. The formulation of specific goals during the first interview keeps counseling on track, and provides clear criteria for evaluating its effectiveness. As suggested in Box 5.3, goals can make or break the success of counseling.

It is easy to sidestep or overlook the client's goals in the counseling process, especially in working with children and adolescents (Murphy & Duncan, 1997). Failures in counseling young people may result from one or more of the following: (1) failing to explicitly discuss goals throughout the counseling process; (2) invalidating or minimizing the student's goal in deference to the goals of the counselor or other adults (Example: "I know you want to work on making more friends, but at this point it is more important to bring your grades up"); and (3) placing one's own theories and positions above those of the student (Example: Despite the student's theory that the school problem is caused by peer difficulties, the counselor continues to probe for deeper intrapsychic causes).

Goal formulation is a cooperative venture in which the counselor accepts and works within the goals and perspectives of the client. Developing goals in collaboration with students, parents, and teachers can be a challenging task. However, it is well worth the effort. Outcome research indicates that success is greatly enhanced when counselors obtain a clear idea of what people want from counseling, and accommodate these goals throughout the counseling process (Marmar et al., 1986; Orlinsky et al., 1994).

Characteristics of Effective Goals. The following considerations are important to keep in mind when formulating goals with students, parents, and teachers.

Specific. In discussing the importance of specific goals, de Shazer (1991) recommends that practitioners encourage clients to "describe how

---

Box 5.3. Goals as Maps

A clear goal is to problem solving what a clear map is to navigation. A good map does not guarantee success, but a poor map, or no map at all, almost always guarantees failure.

---

they will know when the problem is solved and to describe who will be doing what to whom, when, and where, after the problem is solved" (p. 112). Students and others may describe goals using broad and abstract phrases such as "higher self-esteem," "more freedom," or "greater maturity." Many people are not used to thinking and talking in goal language. With some gentle assistance, however, most people are able to develop specific goals. When clients provide vague and abstract descriptions of what they want from counseling, school practitioners can assist them in formulating specific goals by asking the following types of questions:

- What will you be doing differently when your self-esteem is higher?
- What kinds of things will the student be doing when she becomes more responsible?
- What do more mature students do that this student is not doing?

Small. Big problems do not always require big solutions. Fisch et al. (1982) recommend "thinking small" in developing counseling goals. Small goals are more realistic and attainable than large and complex goals, and better suited to the realities of school counseling. Small goals also help practitioners and clients recognize subtle yet important changes in the problem. In solution-focused counseling, small successes are the building blocks for larger changes in school problems. Instead of shooting for the mountaintop all at once, counselors can encourage students and others to focus on the first small step, then the next one, and so on. The following case illustrates the benefits of a modest counseling goal, and the notion that big problems do not always require big solutions.

Case Example: Keeping It Small and Simple. Gary, a seventh-grade student, was referred by his mother, Brenda, for peer problems and classroom misbehavior. The counselor asked Brenda the following question early in the first meeting: "What will be the first small sign that things are getting better for Gary at school?" This presuppositional question was intended to convey a positive expectancy of change, and to encourage Brenda to think small. She replied that he would start attending more carefully to his hygiene.

At the counselor's invitation, Gary agreed to try an experiment during the next week in which he would comb his hair and keep his shirt tucked in at school, and observe any changes in the way he was treated by peers or teachers. He reported that his teachers treated him about the same, but that his classmates were "a little nicer" than usual. Gary continued the experiment the next week, and observed that his teachers began treating him better. Disciplinary referrals at school decreased by about 50 percent during the following month. This case illustrates how one small change can lead to larger, more meaningful changes in a school problem.

Positive. Effective goals are stated as the start or presence of something desirable rather than the end or absence of something undesirable (de Shazer,

1991). When faced with a difficult school problem, it is common for counselors and others to focus on getting rid of it. As de Shazer (1991) points out, "getting rid of something is difficult; the absence of something is hard to know. . . . It is, of course, much easier to know that something different is present" (p. 110).

Research in cognitive psychology indicates that it is easier for people to recognize the presence or "positive instance" of an event or concept than it is to recognize its absence (Jones, 1968; Lefton, 1994). Consider how difficult it is to observe the "absence" of low self-esteem, immaturity, or depression. It is more productive to state goals in a positive form, as the start or presence of something desirable. Stating goals in a positive form reinforces the approach's emphasis on future solutions rather than past problems.

Meaningful. The most important characteristic of an effective goal is that it is meaningful and relevant to the client. In discussing situations in which students are labeled "resistant" or "unmotivated," Durrant (1995) offers the following perspective: "We are all most likely to be motivated to work towards goals that we have set and are therefore meaningful for us, and least likely to be motivated to work on goals imposed by someone else" (p. 59).

Students who enter counseling as visitors may not be very interested in developing goals, or in working toward goals defined by others. Because any attempt to convince them otherwise usually makes matters worse, it is more productive to find something they *are* willing to work on. Framing a question or conversation in a way that respects and acknowledges the student's position instead of challenging it helps to establish rapport and get the ball rolling with a "reluctant" student. Consider the following such question: How will you know when you don't have to come here anymore? This question is particularly useful with students who are required or mandated to attend counseling by school administrators, parents, or the court system. It helps students reflect upon and clarify *their* school-related goals, which are often obscured by their own persistent efforts to maintain and defend their position against the criticism of others. The counselor's cooperation allows students to shift their attention and energies from defending their position to considering what they really want and how they might go about getting it.

Case Example: Mario's Meaningful Goal. Mario, a 10th-grade student, was very angry with his teachers and the school principal. He perceived them as unfair and "out to get him" at school. Mario said that the principal and most of his teachers thought he was "a lazy waste." He stated that the principal and teachers were prejudiced, and that their negative reaction to him was based largely on the stereotype that Hispanics are "dumb and lazy." The counselor inquired about the bases of his perceptions of prejudice, and Mario explained that he and his parents experienced such stereotyping since coming to the United States 2 years ago. When asked what he wanted to change regarding school, Mario asserted that he would *not* change in school because he did not care what they thought of him. He added that he was not about to give in to their demands and "control games." For Mario, improving his school behavior represented "selling out" his cultural heritage and "giving in" to people that he did not respect.

Instead of arguing with Mario about his characterization of the teachers and principal or challenging his cultural perceptions, the counselor accepted his position and posed the following question: "What kinds of things might prove them wrong about you?" This question acknowledged Mario's anger and provided an opportunity for him to change in school in order to prove them wrong. Mario's motivation to prove them wrong was utilized to formulate specific goals regarding his school behavior. These goals were stated in his language and in ways that were personally meaningful to him.

When several different people are involved in counseling regarding the same problem, it is important to encourage goals that are complementary or compatible, even though each goal may be worded differently. This is not as difficult as it sounds. In Mario's case, the behaviors required to meet his goals were the same behaviors required to meet the goals of the teachers and the principal. Similarly, parents may define "responsible behavior" in much the same way that a teenager defines "what it will take to gain more car privileges and freedom at home."

These examples highlight the importance of accepting and working within the position and language of clients while developing goals. Had Mario been asked to work on the goal of "being a better student" or "not getting into as much trouble," he would not have been as motivated to make the changes that he eventually made in his school behavior.

Table 5.2 summarizes the characteristics of effective goals.

Scaling and Miracle Questions. The following section illustrates two types of useful questions for assisting students, parents, and teachers in developing counseling goals. Scaling and miracle questions may be used at various times and for different purposes in solution-focused counseling. They are described in this section because they are particularly relevant to the formulation of goals.

Scaling Questions. The following scaling questions are useful in initial interviews for the purpose of helping people develop clear goals.

- On a scale from 1 to 10, with 1 being "the very worst that things could be," and 10 being "the very best that things could be," where would you rate things in your science class right now? What would the next highest number look like? [Request a "videotalk description" of the next highest number.]
- If a score of 1 is "where things are right now," and 10 is "where you want things to be when we finish counseling," what would a 2 or 3 look like?

Table 5.2. Characteristics of Effective Goals

Characteristic	Description	Useful Questions
Specific	Clear, concrete, specific, observable	What will you be doing differently when you have "higher self-esteem?" What kinds of things will be different when things start improving?
Small	Modest, realistic, reasonable, attainable	What will be the first small sign that things are getting better at school? You said that things in math class were at a 4 on a scale from 1 to 10. What will a 5 look like?
Positive	Stated as the presence of something desirable rather than the absence of something undesirable	What will you be doing *instead of* being depressed? What should this student be doing in your class *instead of* goofing off?
Meaningful	Relevant and important to the client	What do you want to accomplish in counseling? What do you think is the most important thing we need to change this situation?

- What will you be doing differently when you move from where you are now at 3, to a 4 or 5? How would your teacher/parent be able to tell you moved up to a 5?

Scaling offers several advantages. First, it encourages clients to view change as a series of small steps instead of an all-or-nothing solution. Second, scaling is an efficient and ongoing strategy for evaluating progress throughout counseling. Students, parents, and teachers can be asked to rate the situation on a weekly basis throughout and following formal counseling. Third, some people respond more positively to scaling questions than to more direct questions about their goals. For those students and adults who are more comfortable and skilled with numbers than with words, scaling offers a valuable means of developing goals and communicating about them throughout counseling. Scales can even be presented visually by drawing a line on paper and asking: "If this bottom part shows where you were when you used to get in a lot of trouble at school, and this top part shows where you would be if things were perfect at school and you never got in trouble, point to where you would put yourself right now." Refer to Kowalski and Kral (1989) for additional discussion and examples of scaling.

The Miracle Question. The miracle question (de Shazer, 1988) is a classic solution-focused interviewing strategy for clarifying goals and encouraging people to focus on future solutions. The following versions of the miracle question often result in clear, concrete goal descriptions.

- Suppose that one night there is a miracle while you are sleeping and this school problem is solved. How would you be able to tell? What would be different? What will you notice the next morning that would tell you that there has been a miracle? What will your [mother, father, teacher, friends, coach] notice that's different?
- If this problem suddenly vanished, what would you be doing tomorrow at school that would be different than what you usually do? What would be the very first sign of this miracle? Then what?
- If someone waved a magic wand and made this problem disappear, how would you be able to tell things were different?
- What would you notice to be different about your daughter/son when this miracle occurred?
- Pretend there are two movies about your life. Movie #1 is about your life with this problem, and Movie #2 is about your life without the problem. I already know a lot about Movie #1. Tell me what Movie #2 would look like. Who would be in it? What would they be doing? What would you be doing differently in Movie #2?

Asking people to imagine and describe life without the problem is a unique and effective way of encouraging concrete, meaningful goals. Most students and adults enjoy the playful nature of miracle questions and respond favorably to them. However, nothing works all the time with every person. Some students may indicate that the question seems silly or does not make sense to them. In these cases, counselors can simply move on and try something else.

In addition to assisting in goal development, the miracle question enhances solutions by inviting people to focus on the details of a better future. A small piece of the miracle that is already happening in the client's life can be viewed as an exception to the problem, and the client can be encouraged to "do more of it." Students, teachers, and parents can also be urged to pretend or act as if the miracle has already occurred.

Final Comment on Goals. The development of clear goals from the outset of counseling is crucial to success. Effective goals keep counseling on track and focused. As the expression goes, "If you don't know where you're going, you probably won't get there."

Exceptions and Other Client Resources

Client factors contribute largely to successful counseling outcomes (Lambert, 1992). Client factors include a person's strengths, successes, and resources. In solution-focused counseling, interventions for school problems are often based on the strengths and resources of students and others with whom we work. The following section presents interviewing strategies for identifying and clarifying relevant successes and resources of students, parents, and teachers.

Exceptions. An *exception* refers to a circumstance in which the problem does not occur, or occurs less frequently or intensely. Identifying and clarifying exceptions is a central focus of solution-focused interviewing. Once an exception is discovered, counselors can encourage the student and others to "do more of it."

Even in bleak situations when people initially report that "nothing" seems to be working or the student "never" has a good day, there are almost always times when things are just a little better than usual. For example, a student whose teacher initially reports that the student "never" does any assignments has more than likely completed some assignment in recent weeks.

It is common for students and others involved in school problems to view the problem as constant and unchanging. de Shazer (1991) observes that "times when the complaint is absent are dismissed as trivial by the client or even remain completely unseen, hidden from the client's view" (p. 58). This statement is applicable to helping professionals as well as clients. Most of us have been trained to be "problem detectives," sniffing out the problem and piecing together the clues that presumably explain it. This approach encourages counselors to be "solution detectives" as well. Exceptions are powerful building blocks to change that remain unnoticed unless we *listen* and *ask* for them in our initial interviews with students, parents, and teachers.

Listening For Exceptions. People often provide clues to exceptions in their descriptions of the problem. It is important for practitioners to listen carefully for exceptions that may be embedded in the client's description of the problem. Consider the following statements:

- My parents *rarely* let me do what I want.
- My daughter is totally bombing in school. She is failing every subject *except* science.
- This student has completed homework *only once* this entire week in my math class.

The italicized words in these statements offer important clues to exceptions. Counselors can expand problem-solving opportunities by remaining alert to what students, teachers, and parents are already doing, if only just a little, toward arriving at a solution.

Asking For Exceptions. Another way to discover exceptions is to ask for them. As mentioned earlier, many people want to describe their concerns regarding the problem during initial interviews. It is very important to allow for this instead of trying to force the issue of exceptions on clients in a way that might be experienced as lacking understanding or patronizing (Cade & O'Hanlon, 1993). It is always a professional judgment call as to how much "problem talk" to engage in. However, the solution-focused approach generally avoids lengthy excavations into the client's deficiencies and problem history. It is possible to invite students and others to consider exceptions to the problem without forcing it on them.

The following questions and requests are useful in eliciting exceptions to the problem:

- When *doesn't* the problem occur?
- When is this problem *absent* or *less noticeable* during the school day?
- Tell me about the times when you and your son discuss school *without* arguing?

People often report desirable changes in the problem prior to the first counseling session (Lawson, 1994; Weiner-Davis et al., 1987) and between subsequent sessions (Reuterlov, Lofgren, Nordstrom, & Ternstrom, in press), *if* they are asked about them. Clients may not spontaneously report precounseling and between-session changes, and these exceptions may go unnoticed unless we explicitly ask about them. The following questions can be used early in the first session to explore *precounseling change*:

- Have things been any better since you called me to set up this meeting?
- Sometimes people notice that things get a little better right after they make the decision to seek counseling. What have you noticed in your situation?

Between-session change can be assessed and encouraged by the following questions and requests:

- What has been better since we last met?
- Have you noticed any improvements in things in the last few days?
- Between now and the next time we meet, pay attention to the things the student does in your class that make things better.
- Between now and our next meeting, pay attention to the things that are happening at school that you want to continue happening.

Elaborating and Clarifying Exceptions. Once an exception is discovered, counselors can encourage people to elaborate on it by inquiring about related circumstances. The same kinds of questions used to clarify problem-related circumstances are helpful in clarifying the events and circumstances surrounding exceptions. A student who misbehaves frequently in every class except science might be asked the following questions to clarify this exception:

- What is different about your science class than your other classes? What else?
- What is different about your science teacher than your other teachers? What else?
- Where do you sit in science class?
- How would you rate your interest in science as compared to your other classes?
- How do you resist the temptation to mess around more in science class?

Questions to parents and teachers might include the following:

- Who is around when things seem to go smoother at home?
- What do you do or say differently when you and the student are getting along better?
- Do the good times occur more in the mornings or afternoons?

Table 5.3 includes additional questions for exploring exceptions to the problem.

Other Client Resources. In addition to exceptions, clients may offer other valuable resources that can be utilized to resolve school problems. These resources include hobbies, interests, family, friends, and competencies

---

Table 5.3. Sample Interview Questions for Exploring Exceptions

Tell me about a time when the problem hasn't occurred, or has been less of a problem.

How is that different from when the problem is occurring?

Who is around during these times?

What are they saying and doing?

If your teachers/parents were here, what would they say is different about you during the times when the problem isn't happening?

What things are happening at school right now that you would like to see continue happening?

What parts of the miracle are already happening, if only just a little?

[As follow-up to a scaling question] Can you think of a time during the last month/year when things were any higher than a "3"? How was that different than now? What were you doing differently during that time? Of the things that you were doing differently, which ones are you doing now, if only just a little?

Has anything changed for the better since you called to schedule this first meeting? What did you do to get that to happen?

What's better since the last time we talked?

---

in other areas of life. This section presents strategies for discovering and clarifying such resources.

Special Talents and Interests. A person's special talents, hobbies, and interests can be explored with the following types of questions:

- What do you enjoy doing in your spare time?
- How might someone finish this sentence about you: "This person is really good at . . . "?
- If we could talk about anything here, what would you want to talk about?

Heroes. Most young people have heroes. Regardless of whether they are real or fictional, a student's heroes can be utilized in creative ways to encourage a different response to the school problem. The following questions are helpful in exploring students' heroes:

- Who are your heroes?

The following questions can be asked about each hero:
- What is it about [hero's name] that you like?
- What do you think [hero's name] would do if faced with this school problem? Would you be willing to try something like that?

Resilience and Coping. For 13 years, I worked for a school district in one of the most economically disadvantaged communities in the United States. I learned a great deal about resilience from the students and families of this community. First, I learned that many people are capable of surviving and succeeding under extremely difficult life circumstances. I also discovered that people who are struggling with a problem are usually doing *something* to prevent the problem from getting even worse.

These lessons taught me to routinely explore people's resilience and coping skills while interviewing them regarding school problems. The following questions are useful in this regard:

- This has been a very difficult problem for you. How have you managed to keep things from getting even worse?
- How have you managed to keep your sanity and hope in the midst of your child's school problems?
- A lot of students who have gone through what you have would have dropped out of school by now. What keeps you coming to school instead of dropping out?
- How do you resist the urge to [drop out of school/mess around more in class/give up when the work gets hard/punch people that tease you] at school?

These questions imply that the client is competent and resilient in dealing with the problem, if only to stop it from getting worse. Regardless of whether or not clients answer these questions, the implication of competence conveys the counselor's respect for their ideas and resources. I have seen many so-called reluctant or difficult students, such as the one in the following example, respond very favorably to these questions and provide valuable information regarding their resilience and coping skills.

Case Example: Why Haven't You Given Up? Jolette, a 17-year-old high school student, was referred for counseling early in her senior year. She was failing two subjects and her school attendance was erratic. Her teacher stated that she was very capable of earning higher grades, but did not apply herself or take school seriously.

Jolette discussed several difficulties in her life during the first session. She did not remember her father, who moved away when she was an infant. She frequently moved back and forth between her mother's house and her uncle's house, changing school systems with each move. These moves typically were prompted by financial hardships of her mother and uncle, and both of them told her on various occasions that they could not afford to keep her. Jolette felt that nobody wanted her because she was "a financial burden." Both households were investigated by the state's social service agencies due to neglect and abuse charges.

Based on Jolette's school records and comments, these difficulties and challenges had been a regular part of her life since she was born. She worked about 35 hours a week at a local restaurant to support herself. She often worked the late shift from midnight to morning. The following conversation occurred in the beginning of the second session.

Counselor: I've thought about our meeting last week, and I have a question for you. With all the hardships you've had to deal with in your life, how have you resisted the temptation to give up on school altogether and just quit?
Jolette: Why would I want to give up? I've got all of the wonderful experiences ahead of me that I'm going to have in my senior year. I've got all of the wonderful things I'm going to learn in college. Why would I give up? If I give up then I'm going to be flipping burgers the rest of my life. I want to make something better for myself. If I ever plan to have children, I would like to have some money built up in the bank for them to go to college.
Counselor: Sounds like you have a lot to look forward to.
Jolette: Definitely.
Counselor: And that helps to keep you going, to keep you hanging in there in school when things get tough, huh?
Jolette: If it were 2 or 3 years ago, I might have given up. You know, I practically did give up.
Counselor: What's different about you now compared to then?

Jolette went on to describe various aspects of her resilient approach to life, which were incorporated into interventions for improving school attendance and grades. The most effective types of interventions for so-called resistant students are those that include and accommodate as much of the student as possible. In Jolette's case, the conversation probably would have ended quickly had more of the same type of questioning and lecturing occurred ("Why do you insist on not doing your school work when you have the skills to do it?; A high school diploma is essential if you want to get a decent job"). Instead, she was complimented on her resilience and asked how she had managed to hang in there without giving up on school. This allowed her the space to develop her own conclusions and goals regarding the importance of school and graduation. Despite continued difficulties at home and school, Jolette passed all but one of her courses, which was just enough for her to graduate.

Social Supports. Whether seeking out a trusted friend or family member, purchasing a self-help book or tape, attending church, or participating in a support group, the fact is that many people reach out for available help when, where, and from whom they can get it. It is useful to explore and utilize these resources in dealing with school problems.

In addition to listening for social support resources in our conversations with students and others, we can directly explore such resources by way of the following questions:

- Who helps you the most in your day-to-day life?
- How does this person help you? What exactly do they do that is helpful?
- Who do you usually seek out, where do you usually go, and what are some of the things you do to help yourself deal with the challenges and hassles of life?
- Are you or your family connected with any places or groups that might help you with this problem?

Counselors can also explore social support resources by directly contacting important people and agencies in the client's life. This might be done by contacting (with the client's consent) a family member, caseworker, friend, pastor, or neighbor in order to discuss the problem and its potential solutions.

Client As Consultant. Another interviewing strategy for tapping client resources is to ask students and others what they think might help improve things in school, as illustrated by the following questions:

- What do you think would help turn this thing around in school?
- If you were the counselor, what would you say to someone who is struggling with this same type of problem?
- What advice would you give to another high school student/parent/ teacher who is dealing with this kind of situation?
- [For people who have had prior counseling experiences] What things about your previous counselor and counseling experience were most helpful to you? What things were least helpful?

I have been amazed at how often students have provided the essential material for successful school interventions *if only* they are asked. Many solution opportunities are missed when students are viewed merely as "keepers" of the problem with little or nothing to offer toward its solution. In this approach, the client is actively invited to contribute to solutions.

Table 5.4 includes additional questions for exploring client resources.

Summary of Exceptions and Other Client Resources. Tapping into the natural repertoire and environment of students, parents, and teachers expedites change and enhances its maintenance. When counseling interventions incorporate the skills, interests, and environmental supports that are a natural part of the student's everyday life, progress is more likely to be maintained after formal counseling ends (Stokes & Baer, 1977). Exploring exceptions and other client resources is a practical way to tap client factors in our interviews with students, parents, and teachers. Berg (1991) effectively summarizes the rationale for including clients as active collaborators in the counseling process by exploring their successes and resources:

> It is always better for the client to come up with her own solutions rather than being told what to do. When it is her own idea, she is more likely to be committed to successful solutions. In addition, if a solution is generated from within the client's existing resources, it fits naturally

---

Table 5.4. Sample Interview Questions for Exploring Other Client Resources

Tell me about something you do well outside of school.

If you could have any kind of job you wanted when you got older, what job would you choose?

What is it about you that would make you good at that job?

Who are your heroes? What do you admire most about them?

How do you manage to "hold it together" with all the trouble that you've had in your life?

How do you keep hanging in there without giving up?

How have you kept things from getting even worse?

As a teacher/parent, how do you stay sane while dealing with this problem day in and day out?

Why haven't you given up?

Who is most helpful to you when you have a problem?

How do you go about getting their help?

If you had a younger brother or sister with this same school problem, what would you say to them about it?

If you were the counselor, what advice would you have for a student who is dealing with this type of problem?

with her way of doing things and it is easier to do more of. Furthermore, when the solution is more congruent with her lifestyle than any newly learned behavior, she is less likely to relapse. (p. 64)

The questions and strategies in this chapter are versatile interviewing tools that can be applied to a broad range of middle and high school problems. These tools can be adapted to fit counselors' unique style, work setting, and clients.

SUMMARY AND CONCLUSIONS

1. Interviewing is a powerful opportunity to discover and clarify solutions. Specific questions were provided for exploring the problem, solution attempts, client position, goals, exceptions, and other client resources. Given the time demands and constraints of school practitioners, it is useful to explore as many of these areas as possible in the first interview.

2. Students, teachers, and parents are encouraged to clearly describe the problem in specific, behavioral terms ("videotalk") instead of using vague, abstract terminology.

3. Exploring people's past and present solution attempts helps counselors to avoid "more of the same" ineffective strategies, as well as providing clues about what may work in changing the problem.

4. Clarifying the client's position helps counselors to structure their comments and questions in cooperative ways that strengthen the client–counselor relationship and enhance change.

5. The formulation of clear goals is perhaps the most underrated yet crucial aspect of solution-focused interviewing. Effective goals are specific, small, positive, and meaningful. Clear goals keep counseling on track and assist in evaluating its effectiveness.

6. Perhaps the most distinctive feature of solution-focused interviewing is the practitioner's assessment of exceptions to the problem and other client resources. The search for exceptions and other resources is guided by the practical notion that it is easier to build on existing successes, interests, and competencies than it is to eliminate problems or teach new behaviors or skills.

This chapter invited counselors to expand their interviewer role from "problem detective" to "solution detective." The focus on utilizing what works for students, teachers, and parents is continued in the next two chapters, which describe interventions based on exceptions to the problem (Chapter 6) and other client resources (Chapter 7).

PRACTICE EXERCISES

1. With a partner in the role of student, parent, or teacher, experiment with the questions listed below to open the first interview. Note any differences

in the responses you get to each of these questions. Ask your partner about any differences in his or her reaction to these questions.

- What is the problem?
- What do you want to see happen as a result of counseling?
- What is the student doing or not doing that you see as the problem?
- What do you hope to accomplish with counseling?

2. Tape record your next counseling session, and review the tape in regard to the amount of "problem talk" and "solution talk." There is no right or wrong percentage of solution talk. However, if the majority of your questions and comments are problem-focused, consider how you could incorporate more solution-focused questions and comments into future sessions.

3. Randomly select a few of your current counseling cases, and ask yourself if the goals in these cases are sufficiently specific, small, positive, and meaningful to the client. If not, consider how the goal might be altered to make it more effective.

4. Think of a situation or problem in your life that you would like to change. What will be the first small sign that things are getting a little better? To practice scaling, rate the problem from 1 to 10, with 1 being "as bad as it can be," and 10 being "as good as it can be." What would the next higher number look like? Be specific in describing what you and others will be doing and saying differently when things start improving. Note any differences in focusing on improvements as compared to focusing on what's wrong with the situation or with you.

5. Select a problem you are currently dealing with in your life. Ask yourself what would be different if a miracle occurred and the problem vanished. How could you tell? Specifically, what would be different in your life? Of those things that would be different, which ones are already happening, if only just a little? What is different about those times when part of the miracle is happening, and what could you do to sustain or increase them?

6

Utilizing Exceptions to the Problem

*A Sufi man was walking along the road when he spotted his friend Mulla searching
for something under the streetlamp outside his house. When the man asked what he
was doing, Mulla said that he was looking for his lost keys. The man got on his
hands and knees and joined Mulla in the search. After several minutes, the man
asked: "Where exactly did you drop them?" "Way over there," replied Mulla,
pointing to a field across the road. "Then why, might I ask, are you looking here?"
"Because the light's so much better here," Mulla said.*

—Adapted from Shah, *The Exploits of the Incomparable Mulla Nasrudin*

Psychology and counseling have traditionally focused on the deficiencies
and weaknesses of clients (de Shazer, 1988). However, counseling outcome research suggests that solutions are more plentiful on the less familiar road of client strengths and resources. Even though "the light may
be better" in the familiar domain of client deficiencies, finding the keys
or solutions is always more important than looking under the light.

The most distinguishing feature of solution-focused counseling is the
emphasis on what is working instead of what is wrong with people. This feature is no more apparent than in the strategy of utilizing exceptions. An *exception* refers to a specific circumstance or situation in which the problem
does not occur, or occurs less often or intensely.

The strategy of utilizing exceptions has evolved largely from work of
Steve de Shazer and colleagues (Berg, 1991; de Shazer, 1985, 1988). From a
practical standpoint, the solution-focused model suggests that it is more efficient to increase existing successes than to eliminate problems. This chapter
describes and illustrates a five-step strategy for utilizing exceptions in working
with school problems (Murphy, 1994b).

THE 5-E METHOD OF UTILIZING EXCEPTIONS

If I focus on a problem, the problem increases, if I focus on the answer, the answer increases.

—Alcoholics Anonymous, *Alcoholics Anonymous Comes of Age*

The process of utilizing exceptions can be broken into five steps. Steps 1 and 2 were addressed in the previous chapter, and are discussed only briefly below in order to describe the entire process.

Step 1: Eliciting

It is common for people involved in problem situations to view the problem as constant and unchanging. Therefore, it is usually necessary to ask questions, assign tasks, or use rating scales and forms to elicit exceptions. Exception-finding questions include the following:

- When is the problem absent or less noticeable during the school day?
- Can you think of a time when the student did a little better this week?
- Of all your classes, which one is the most tolerable?

The miracle question (see Chapter 5) can also be used to elicit exceptions. When students, parents, or teachers describe life without the problem in response to the miracle question, they can be asked to describe those aspects of the miracle that are already happening, that is, exceptions.

If no exceptions are identified by way of direct questions, clients can be given tasks. The following variations of the "formula first session task" (de Shazer, 1985) are useful in eliciting exceptions to school problems.

- Between now and next week when we meet, make a list of the things [in your life/at school/in a particular class] that you would like to see continue.
- Pay attention to the times you are able to resist the urge to [hit someone/skip school when you feel like it/or whatever the problem is].
- Observe when the problem is not occurring or is just a little better, and pay attention to how you are able to make that happen.

Rating scales and surveys can also be completed by students, parents, and teachers in order to elicit exceptions. Most school-related rating scales and questionnaires are heavily problem focused. For example, a teacher or parent might be asked to rate the student on the extent to which he or she demonstrates various problems such as depression, anxiety, or hyperactivity. Although these scales are designed primarily to detect and explore the student's deficits and problems, exceptions might be identified by examining those items that are scored as "less problematic" than others.

Counselors can elicit exceptions in a more direct way be using instruments that are solution focused instead of problem focused. Appendix C provides two such examples. The Solution Identification Scale (S-Id) is a behavioral checklist developed by Kral (1988) to detect positive, desirable behaviors on the part of the student. Although the scale was originally designed to be completed by teachers and parents, high school students can also be asked to complete it. Unlike problem-focused scales, the S-Id invites people to focus on a student's competencies and successes. Counselors can utilize the S-Id by exploring the details and circumstances surrounding positive behaviors noted in items marked "very much" or "pretty much."

Appendix C also includes the Quick Survey, an open-ended questionnaire that I developed for teachers to complete on students referred for counseling. In middle and high schools, this could be given to as many of the student's teachers who are willing to complete it. The solution-focused nature of the survey encourages teachers to pay attention to exceptions and related circumstances. The Quick Survey can also be adapted for parents to gather information about exceptions outside the school setting.

Unlike most other ratings scales and surveys, these instruments are not "scored" or used to compare the student's performance to that of his or her peers. These are interventive versus diagnostic tools used to help counselors and clients devise interventions based on exceptions to the school problem.

Step 2: Elaborating

Once identified, the exception can be elaborated or clarified by asking about related features and circumstances. Chapter 5 provided numerous questions for elaborating upon exceptions, such as "What is different about [those times/that class/or whatever the exception is]?" It is important to obtain detailed information about the circumstances surrounding the exception before moving to the next step. Details and features of the "exception context" provide direction for exception-based interventions in Step 3.

Step 3: Expanding

This is the intervention phase and the heart of the 5-E process in which the student, teacher, or parent is encouraged to expand the exception to other situations or settings, or to a greater frequency.

To Other Situations or Settings. As an example of expanding the exception to other situations or settings, consider the student who behaves more acceptably in science class than in any other class. Upon discovering that science was the only class in which the student sat close to the teacher and the chalkboard, the counselor can encourage the student to sit closer to the teacher in another class or two. As simple as this sounds, improvements in school problems frequently result from expanding "what works" in one situation to another situation, then another, and so on.

To a Greater Frequency. In addition to expanding exceptions to different situations or settings, people can be encouraged to "do the exception" more frequently. I recall such an example involving a ninth-grade biology teacher who requested help in managing the behavior of his entire class. When asked about times or activities when things seemed to go a little smoother in class, he reported fewer behavior problems (the exception) during small-group activities and experiments (the exception context). I suggested that he consider doing more activities and experiments in class, providing that course objectives could still be met while doing so. When I saw the teacher the next month, he commented that things were much better and that he was doing some type of special activity almost every day.

Another noteworthy aspect of this case was that the teacher modified the suggested intervention in two creative ways. First, he scheduled group activities and experiments during the last half of the class whenever possible, because classroom behavior had typically been worse during the latter portion of class. Second, he offered certain special activities as rewards contingent upon acceptable classroom behavior during the entire week. In solution-focused counseling, clients are encouraged to adapt interventions to fit their unique style and circumstances. This case illustrates the simple yet effective strategy of urging people to do more of what is already working for them.

Step 4: Evaluating

Evaluation of exception-based interventions, as well as other solution-focused interventions, is based primarily on the client's judgment of goal attainment. Many of the evaluation strategies recommended in the professional literature are impractical for busy school practitioners. As scientifically sound and rigorous as an evaluation method may be, it is useless unless it is used. Therefore, the following discussion presents methods that are both practical and compatible with the solution-focused approach.

Scaling Techniques. Scaling questions are very useful in evaluating the effectiveness of counseling. Students and others can be asked the following question on a regular basis throughout the counseling process: "On a scale of 1 to 10, with 1 being 'the worst' and 10 'the best', how would you rate the problem during the past week?"

Paper-and-Pencil Methods. Paper-and-pencil methods can also be employed to evaluate the effectiveness of counseling interventions by asking students, parents, and teachers to complete rating scales, checklists, inventories, or questionnaires. For example, a parent and teacher could fill out a behavior rating scale on a student before and after counseling, and the two sets of ratings could be compared to assess their perceptions of improvement. Although marketed rating scales can be used for this purpose, practitioners can also design short, user-friendly rating scales that are specifically tailored to the content and goal of counseling. Table 6.1 provides an example of a teacher rating scale that was developed for a case in which the goal was to improve the student's classroom behavior and to increase assignment completion. The scale

Table 6.1. Individually Developed Teacher Rating Scale for Evaluating Progress

Student: <u>Jerry Smith</u>   Teacher/Class: <u>Ms. McCreary/Science</u>   Date: <u>4/9/97</u>

1. On a scale of 1 to 10, with 1 being "the worst it can be" and 10 being "the best it can be," rate Jerry's behavior in your class during the past week: ____

2. As compared to when the referral for counseling was made, Jerry's current behavior in your class is: ____better   ____worse   ____about the same.

   If better, what is he doing differently now that's better?

   _____

   _____

3. As compared to when the referral for counseling was made, Jerry's completion of in-class assignments during the past week was: ____better   ____worse ____about the same.

4. As compared to when the referral for counseling was made, Jerry's completion of homework assignments for your class during the past week was: ____better ____worse   ____about the same.

5. Please list the things that Jerry is *already doing* to improve his behavior and assignment completion in your class (other than what is listed above).

   _____

   _____

6. Please list the things that Jerry *could do differently* to improve his behavior and assignment completion in your class.

   _____

   _____

7. Add *any other comments or questions* that are important for me to consider in dealing with this situation.

   _____

   _____

THANK YOU FOR YOUR COOPERATION.

took about 10 minutes to design and type up, and about 5 minutes for teachers to complete. All five of the student's teachers completed the scale four separate times during the 2-month counseling period in order to provide an ongoing snapshot of the student's progress in each class.

Permanent Products. Examination of permanent products, such as report cards and discipline records, is another practical way of evaluating the effectiveness of intervention. For example, comparison of report cards and discipline records before, during, and following counseling could be used to evaluate the student's goal of earning passing grades and increasing the number of days without detention. Additional permanent products include classroom work samples, homework assignments, midterm progress reports, teachers' grade books, and students' cumulative files.

Single-Case Evaluation Designs. Single-case evaluation designs (Barlow, Hayes, & Nelson, 1984) can be used in conjunction with the methods above to evaluate progress. The most practical of these designs is the "AB" design, in which A is the baseline phase and B is the intervention phase (Kazdin, 1994). For example, a teacher might rate or "scale" a student's daily classroom behavior for a week or so before intervention (the A phase) and for several weeks following it (the B phase). One major advantage of this type of evaluation is that it provides ongoing repeated measures of progress. Ongoing repeated measures are more comprehensive and informative than one or two occasional measures throughout the course of counseling. Additional applications of single-case designs for evaluating school interventions can be found elsewhere (Conoley, 1987; Kratochwill & Bergan, 1990; Murphy, 1992).

Step 5: Empowering

When improvements in the school problem are noted, the emphasis shifts toward "keeping the ball rolling" by empowering these changes and helping people maintain them. The maintenance of treatment gains has been extensively covered in the literature. This section is not an exhaustive review of all possible maintenance techniques, but an overview of strategies that are particularly compatible with solution-focused counseling.

Solution-focused counseling "begins with the end in mind" by routinely employing maintenance strategies throughout the counseling process. Like evaluation techniques, methods for maintaining progress must be time-effective and practical to accommodate the daily realities of school practitioners and their clients.

Collaborating. Collaborating with clients throughout the counseling process is one of the surest ways to promote ownership and maintenance of desired changes. One way to do this is by offering suggestions and ideas instead of telling people what to do, as illustrated in the following example: "What would you think about approaching a couple of your teachers and asking them how you might improve your grades?" Students, teachers, and parents who perceive their role in the counseling process as active and important are more likely to take personal ownership of desired changes, and to continue to apply effective interventions on their own (Reinking et al., 1978).

Blaming the Client. A similar maintenance strategy is "blaming the client" for successful changes (Kral, 1986). People may attribute progress to pure luck, assuming very little personal credit for bringing it about. This approach seeks to increase clients' sense of "personal agency" (White & Epston, 1990). Students, parents, and teachers are more likely to maintain improvements when they are considered to be the result of something *they* did, and can do again in the future. The following questions are useful in blaming clients for success in order to increase their ownership for the change, and help them clarify what they did to bring it about:

- What are you doing differently now to make it through math class for a whole week without getting kicked out?
- How did you manage to get your daughter to school on time for the past 3 days?
- What does this tell you about yourself? What do you think this tells your parents and teachers about you?

Clarifying Intentions and Plans. Clarifying and empowering the client's intentions and plans to sustain progress is another useful way to keep the ball rolling after improvements have been noted. Counselors can help students and others clarify their intentions and plans for maintaining progress by asking variations of the question, "How are you going to maintain these changes?" In addition to helping clients clarify their intentions to maintain improvements, the following questions convey the counselor's confidence in their ability to do so:

- Do you plan to continue these changes in the way you act at school? Why is it important for you to do this?
- What can you do to continue the progress you have made with this student in your math class?
- How are you going to stick with this plan in the future?

Clarifying the Impact of Change. Clarifying the impact of positive changes on the client's life is useful in helping students and others maintain such improvements. Upon learning about a desired change in a school problem, it is useful to inquire about the "ripple effects" of this change in other areas of school and life. Consider the following questions in this regard:

- How do your parents and teachers treat you differently now that you've made these changes?
- What effect have these changes had on your confidence and self-esteem?
- Have you noticed any other positive changes or differences in the way you and your son get along since you began asking him fewer questions about school?

- I know that Monique's classroom behavior has improved since you began meeting individually with her for a few minutes on Friday afternoons. Have you noticed any other benefits of these Friday meetings?

Preparing for Relapse. Although people are naturally relieved by desired changes, some clients may fear that improvements will not last. In these cases, counselors can empathize with clients' apprehension by suggesting that occasional slips are an inevitable part of the change process. Clients who are prepared for the possibility of relapse are likely to respond in effective ways when slips occur. Without such preparation, people may exaggerate the significance of a relapse and respond to it in unproductive ways. For example, parents or teachers who are not adequately prepared for a relapse may respond to it by reverting back to the same ineffective parenting or teaching strategies that contributed to the original problem. The following questions help students, parents, and teachers prepare for relapse:

- What will you do if you notice your grades slipping in social studies class?
- What will you do the next time your son does not get up for school?
- How will you handle it if this new classroom management plan stops working as well as it has been?

Allowing Clients to Advise Others. Another way to empower desired changes is to ask clients what advice they would give others who wish to make the kinds of changes that they have recently made. When clients are asked to help the counselor help others, it often prompts them to further reflect upon what they did to bring about desired changes in the school problem. Enlisting clients as consultants in this way conveys respect for their ideas and competencies, which may enhance their confidence in maintaining desired changes. In addition to asking people for suggestions, counselors can have clients write out their "success stories" for the counselor and others to consult in the future. The counselor's request for such stories can be structured in a general way ("Write a story about how you made these changes") or in a more specific way ("Write a list of what other seventh-grade students could do in the classroom and at home to improve their grades"). I have also invited students who have made successful changes to become members of the Consultant Club, a group consisting of former clients who have agreed to let me call on them in the future for ideas and suggestions for other students. Students who join the Consultant Club are given a membership certificate. As discussed next, the use of certificates and other documents can be used to recognize and empower successful changes.

Documents. Documents such as letters, awards, and certificates can be routinely incorporated into the counseling process to reinforce and maintain progress. White and Epston (1990) provide numerous examples of how documents can be used to empower clients' progress and victories over the problem. Middle and high school students respond very positively to specific notes and letters. The following letter was sent to a sixth-grade student after she had made significant improvements in school behavior.

Dear Denise,

Congratulations on the changes you have made this week in your school behavior. I know how hard it was to resist the urge to mess around in class, but you did it. I would like to learn more about how you made these changes. I will ask you how you did it the next time we meet.

Appendix D displays some letters and other documents that can be used to help students clarify and maintain positive changes in school problems.

Leaving the Door Open. Another way to empower and maintain progress is by "leaving the door open" for follow-up visits and booster sessions at the request of the student, parent, or teacher. Although solution-focused counseling conveys confidence in people's ability to maintain changes, it is useful to offer clients the opportunity for follow-up contacts that may help them sustain progress. When goals are reached and formal counseling ends, counselors can offer follow-up booster sessions or phone calls to check on progress and encourage people to continue doing what works.

The 5-E Method, summarized in Table 6.2, is a systematic strategy for utilizing exceptions in dealing with a variety of middle and high school problems. The strategy of working with what works is illustrated in the following cases.

CASE EXAMPLES OF UTILIZING EXCEPTIONS

In addition to demonstrating the technique of utilizing exceptions, these cases illustrate the cooperative, collaborative nature of solution-focused counseling. Dialogue and commentary are provided periodically in order to illustrate clearly the counseling process.

The Exceptional Quarter

Jeff was referred by his teachers for evaluation at the end of his fifth-grade school year. The teachers requested the evaluation in order to determine his eligibility for placement in an alternative school for students with behavioral disabilities. Referral concerns included the following: (a) talking out in class loudly, frequently, and without permission; (b) refusal to complete academic assignments; and (c) peer relationship problems. His mother, teacher, and school principal reported that these problems had occurred throughout the school year, but were particularly evident during the last 2 months of the year.

The following excerpts are from the first interview with Jeff and his mother (Ms. S) a few weeks after the school year ended. In the beginning of the interview, Jeff said that he wanted to do better in school, but that the

Table 6.2. The 5-E Method of Utilizing Exceptions

Step 1: Eliciting
Listen for and ask about exceptions.
Examples: In what class is the problem absent or less noticeable?; Tell me about a time you made it through the whole day without getting kicked out of class; Observe and make a note of the times when the problem is not occurring or is just a little better.

Step 2: Elaborating
Explore conditions and circumstances related to the exception.
Examples: How is your math class different than the classes you are having more problems with?; During what type of class activities does this student behave better?

Step 3: Expanding
Encourage the student, teacher, or parent to do "more of" the exception.
Examples: Since you get to school on time when your brother wakes you, is it possible for him to start waking you more often?; It might be fun to try an experiment this week where you do more "science class behavior" in one or two of the classes you're having trouble with, and observe any differences in the way your teachers treat you.

Step 4: Evaluating
Assist the student, teacher, or parent in evaluating progress by using some or all of the following strategies: scaling techniques, paper-and-pencil methods, permanent products, and single-case evaluation designs.
Examples: On a scale of 1 to 10, with 1 being "the worst it could be," and 10 being "the best it could be," where would you rate your behavior in math class during the past week?; Would you say things are about the same, better, or worse than they were before you began this new strategy with the student?; Examine school attendance records for the past month to assess the student's progress on the goal of arriving to school on time.

Step 5: Empowering
Assist the student, teacher, or parent in empowering and maintaining desired changes in the problem by collaborating versus dictating, blaming the client, clarifying intentions and plans, clarifying the impact of change, preparing for relapse, allowing clients to advise others, documents, and leaving the door open for follow-up contacts.
Examples: How are you planning to continue with these changes?; What will you do when you have a bad day or things slip a bit?; Now that you have made things better for yourself in school, what would you say to another student/parent/teacher who is dealing with the same type of situation?

---

teachers and principal "made it impossible." The dialogue picks up with the counselor's attempt to elicit an exception to the problem.

Counselor: What kinds of things help you hang in there in school?
Jeff: Nothing. Well, maybe the after-school program where we get to play basketball in the gym.

Counselor: Mmm. Tell me about that. I'm not familiar with that.

[*The counselor conveys the ambassador perspective by being curious and requesting Jeff's help in clarifying previous solution attempts and exceptions to the problem.*]

Jeff: Once a week, any kids that want to stay after school and play basketball or volleyball.

[*Jeff's perception of what has worked, or might work, is an important consideration in developing interventions that will be acceptable to him. A few minutes later, the counselor explores goals by asking the miracle question.*]

Counselor: If there was a miracle that happened tonight while you were sleeping, and all these school problems just vanished, what would be different when you went into school, or when you woke up in the morning? Ms. S [mother], please jump right in too.

Ms. S: He won't holler and scream. He won't mistreat his teachers. He won't mistreat the office staff. And I won't be called up there every other day.

Counselor: What else?

Ms. S: He'll start participating in school activities, and his grades will be decent. I'm not saying A's or B's, but not straight F's.

Counselor: So his grades will be certainly better than . . . ?

Ms. S: At least a C average.

Counselor: Jeff, what else will show you that things are going better in school?

Jeff: I don't know.

Counselor: Ms. S, back to your statement of "he won't mistreat people," can you tell me what that will look like? Give me some examples of that.

[*The counselor requests a "videotalk description" to clarify exactly what Jeff's mother means by the phrase "won't mistreat people." The next excerpt picks up a few minutes later, after Jeff said that he spent a large amount of time in the principal's office instead of in class last year.*]

Counselor: Which did you like better, being in the office or being in class?

Jeff: Class.

Counselor: Why?

[*Jeff explains the advantages of being in class instead of the office. Most of his comments pertain to what he does not like about the office instead of what he likes about class. The next excerpt occurred about 20 minutes into the interview, following Jeff's comment that "school doesn't really bother me." This statement stood out from Jeff's overall negative description of school. The counselor follows this lead by asking Jeff what he liked about school, as illustrated below.*]

Counselor: What is it about school that you like?

Jeff: I like math, I like spelling, and I like science.

Counselor: Math, spelling, and science. Of those three, which one do you like the best?

Jeff: Math.

Counselor: What's your favorite thing about it?

[*The focus of the interview continues to shift from descriptions of the problem, and of what Jeff does not like, to exceptions and competencies that might be employed to help him reach his goal of staying in class more often.*]

Counselor: Jeff, can you think of a day this year that you stayed in class all day and weren't sent to the office?

[*This question is directly designed to elicit an exception.*]

Jeff: Yeah. The whole second quarter when they gave the special award. I made C's and B's.

Counselor: How would you explain that?

Jeff: The teacher gave this special award.

Counselor: What kind of award?

[*The interview proceeded to elaborate the details of the special award and other aspects of this exception, such as the specific things that Jeff did differently during the second quarter to help himself get better grades and stay in class more often. In addition to exploring this exception, Jeff and his mother were asked to make a written list of anything that would help him reach his goal of improving school behavior. The interview concluded with compliments to Jeff and his mother for their sustained effort and courage in trying to improve things, and for making the effort to attend the meeting in the summer.*]

Examination of school records confirmed Jeff's report of behavioral and academic improvements during the second quarter. Jeff had 43 documented disciplinary infractions during the school year, only one of which occurred during the second quarter. He earned an average grade of C for the second quarter as compared to D for each of the other three quarters. Upon entering the new school year, interventions were developed to encourage Jeff and others to do more of what had already worked during the "second quarter exception." Interventions included adaptations of the special award, and Jeff's regular participation in the after-school program. Jeff was also encouraged to do some of the other things that he said had helped him do better in school. For instance, he said it was helpful to remind himself that he did not want to repeat a grade in school. Therefore, it was recommended that he remind himself of this upon entering the school building each morning. These interventions were implemented in his regular school instead of an alternative placement, with the agreement that alternatives would be considered if his progress during the first quarter of the year was unsatisfactory.

Jeff's grades and behavior were significantly better during the first quarter of the new year as compared to the previous year. No disciplinary infractions were recorded during the first 2 months of school, and he earned a grade average of B. His teachers and principal commented that he was "doing great" and that he had made "a major turnaround" in school behavior. Two meetings were held with Jeff during the first quarter of the sixth grade for the purpose of empowering and maintaining desired changes, as illustrated in the following excerpt.

Counselor: Things seem to be on track for your goal of passing to the seventh grade. A lot different than last year. What are you doing differently to make this happen?

[*This question seeks to empower progress by exploring what Jeff did to bring it about, that is, by "blaming the client" for success.*]

Jeff: Well, I'm doing my work without complaining. I'm listening to the teacher. I'm not smarting off like I used to, because it just gets you in trouble. I'm tired of being in trouble. I was in too much trouble last year.

[*The counselor and Jeff further explored how he was able to "do work without complaining, listen to the teacher, and not smart off like he used to." They also discussed his intentions and plans to continue such efforts.*]

Academic and behavioral progress was consistently maintained throughout the entire school year, and Jeff successfully passed to seventh grade. The following letter was sent at the end of the year to further acknowledge and empower successful changes in school behavior:

> Dear Jeff: I want to congratulate you on the improvements you have made in school behavior this year. I know it took hard work to make these improvements. I admire the fact that you hung in there and didn't give up during the tough times this year. That takes courage. Way to go, Jeff!

Jeff was also invited to participate in the counselor's Consultant Club in order to provide suggestions for other students who may experience school difficulties similar to the ones that he overcame. He readily accepted the invitation.

Discussion. This case illustrates the value of building on successes to resolve school problems. Whereas previous interventions and discussions had focused on *why* Jeff acted out, and on other aspects of what was wrong with him, the counselor focused on discovering and building on *what worked* for Jeff. Once the second quarter exception was discovered, Jeff and the school staff simply did more of it with very favorable results.

The Competent Test-Anxiety Group

This example describes the strategy of utilizing exceptions in group counseling. A total of five female students in grades 10 and 11 participated in a six-session "test-anxiety" counseling group. Solution-focused strategies were used in conjunction with educational and skill-building activities such as study strategies, test-taking tips, and relaxation exercises.

During the first meeting, students completed some basic information forms and responded to questions about what they hoped to gain from the group. Their goals included improved test performance, better study habits, and less worry and tension before important tests.

The following requests were presented at the beginning of the second session in order to explore what students were already doing toward their stated goals, that is, to identify exceptions to their test-anxiety problems.

- Tell me about a test within the last month or so that you did a little better on. What subject area was the test in? What was different about this test than other tests? What was different about the way you prepared for the test? What did you do differently right before the test? What did you do differently during the test?
- Think of a recent test that you were able to study pretty effectively for. How did you study for the test? What was different about the way you studied?
- Think about a recent test you had that you worried a little less about. How did you manage to do that? What does that tell you about yourself?

Details and conditions related to these exceptions were explored during the second group session. The students seemed to appreciate the opportunity to discuss things that they were already doing to help themselves. One student commented, "I thought I was doing *everything* wrong." Students were also asked to share strategies that they thought about doing, but had not yet tried, and strategies that they thought would help them, but were not willing to try at the time. At the end of the second meeting, students were given the formula first-session task session (de Shazer, 1985) as follows: "Between now and our next meeting in 2 weeks, observe and list those things you are already doing, to prepare for and take tests, that you want to continue doing."

As is often the case when students are asked to consult on their own problems, the strategies generated by these five students were very similar to test-anxiety interventions from the professional literature. In subsequent meetings, the educational materials on test-taking, relaxing, and studying were integrated with student-generated ideas and strategies on these topics. The last three meetings opened with the following question designed to elicit and explore between-session improvements: "What's better since our last meeting?"

Data on the students' test performance and grades indicated that the group was successful. Four of the five students increased their overall grade point average, and all five students reported improvements in test-taking skills on a self-report questionnaire. The comments that students made following the group's termination were also encouraging. Comments relevant to the solution-focused approach included the following:

- I realized that I had good ideas, even if I wasn't using them all the time.
- It was cool when we rattled off all those ideas, and I used some of them.
- It was good to get ideas from other students for a change, instead of the teacher.
- I started doing better on tests when I did the stuff I said I needed to do.

The Student for Whom Nothing Was Going Right

Joel, a 10th-grade student in advanced classes, was referred because his grades (C's and D's) were considerably below his ability level. The following dialogue took place early in the first meeting with Joel.

Joel: Nothing is going right for me.
[*The perception that nothing is going right is a common one for clients who are dealing with a significant problem. In these cases, it is helpful to acknowledge the client's experience before rushing into questions about exceptions.*]
Counselor: That stinks.
Joel: I'll say.

Joel went on to say that he had difficulty concentrating in class, and that he was upset with some problems between him and his father. He added that he felt "pretty depressed" about things in general, and that he wanted to do better in school. He talked about various things that were bothering him, including problems with his girlfriend and with some of his other friends. Here's what happened next.

Joel: I don't know what's going on with me. I wish I could just snap out of it.
Counselor: What would you be doing differently if you snapped out of it?
Joel: I don't know. I'd just be happier. I'd be doing my school work like usual.
Counselor: Okay. So you'd be doing your school work and you'd be happier. That makes sense. If I followed you around with a video camera and filmed you being happier, what other things would I see you doing?
[*The counselor uses Joel's own language ("snap out of it" and "happy") to obtain a video description of what he wants to be doing differently in place of the problem.*]
Joel: When I'm happy, I kid around more with my friends. I make stupid jokes. Everybody tells me I'm funny.
Counselor: Do you like it when people tell you you're funny?
Joel: Yeah. It makes me feel good because I can cheer them up by cracking jokes.
Counselor: That's a good skill. You know any good jokes you can tell me?
Joel: Not really.
Counselor: They're not all dirty, are they?
Joel: [*smiles*] Not all of them. In fact, most of them aren't.
Counselor: Wow. That's impressive. It's impressive that you can entertain a group of teenagers with jokes that are mostly clean. You should write a book about that.
Joel: [*smiles*] Maybe I will.
[*Selekman (1993) suggests that humor is an important strategy for engaging adolescents in the counseling process. However, humor can backfire if it is not done with respect for the client's unique style and circumstance. If done respectfully, humor provides a way to introduce some flexibility and playfulness into problem situations that are viewed with grim, determined seriousness.*]

At the close of the meeting, the counselor presented the formula first session task (de Shazer, 1985) as described below.

Counselor: I really appreciate you sharing stuff here. It takes some courage to talk about yourself to someone you just met. I feel like I've got a pretty good handle on the things you're concerned about. I'm going to ask you to do something during the next 2 weeks that would help me learn more about the things in your life that you want to see continue happening. I'd like you to make a list of the things in your life that you want to see continue. This will help me learn more about you and your situation. When we meet in 2 weeks, we can look at your list and take things from there.

[*This task invited Joel to consider exceptions to the dominant view that nothing is going right. The formula first session task does not directly challenge people's experience of the problem situation, but merely invites them to take another look at things through a solution-focused lens.*]

Joel returned in 2 weeks with a long list, and said that making the list helped him realize that he had a lot of things going for him. Joel's list included several exceptions to the notion that nothing was going right for him. He said that he appreciated his sense of humor (Exception #1). He also wanted to continue having many friends, especially close friends with whom he could talk about anything (Exception #2). He expressed the desire to continue getting along well with a couple of his teachers (Exception #3), and said that he probably needed to work harder in their classes in order to "stay in their good graces."

Additional exceptions were identified by asking Joel some between-session questions regarding what else was better since the previous meeting. Joel said that he finally confronted his father about several recent promises that his father had made and broken (Exception #4). His father told him that he would be more thoughtful in the future (Exception #5). Joel also reported that he was dating a new girl (Exception #6), and that he was able to concentrate better in class (Exception #7). While reading some stories for English class about different cultures, Joel was impressed by the following message in one of the stories: No matter how hard you try, you can never have complete and total happiness. This helped him relax and enjoy things more, even when he was not as happy as he would like to be (Exception #8).

The details of these exceptions were explored, and Joel was encouraged to keep doing them in the future. He chose to work primarily on relating more effectively to his father and doing better in his classes. The conversation ended in the following way.

Counselor: So what can you do to make this stuff keep happening?

[*Clients sometimes enter counseling blaming others for the problem, and waiting for others to change in order to resolve it. Questions about what they have already* done, or plan to do to make things better, are useful in conveying their own responsibility and personal agency in their lives.]

Joel: I guess I can just keep concentrating in school. With my Dad, I guess I'll just talk to him whenever we're having problems.
Counselor: Remind me about what you used to do when the two of you had problems.
[Talking about the problem in the past tense empowers desired changes by conveying the notion of "that was then, and this is now."]

Joel's schoolwork improved, and no additional concerns were noted throughout the remainder of the school year. The following excerpt is from a brief meeting with Joel about 1 month before the school year ended.

Counselor: You've really made some heavy duty changes in your life, haven't you?
[This questions blames Joel for success in order to enhance his ownership for desired changes.]
Joel: Yeah. It seems like it.
Counselor: What does making these changes tell you about yourself?
Joel: It tells me it was up to me all along. I guess I knew that, but I really didn't believe it.
Counselor: Does it change the way you view yourself?
Joel: Yes.
Counselor: How so?
Joel: It makes me feel good. It makes me realize that I can do it. I can change if I want to.
Counselor: Have you noticed any differences in the way your parents and teachers treat you since you made these changes?
[Sometimes students are unaware of the impact and ripple effects that positive changes can have in their lives, including effects on their self-image, and on the responses of other people. These questions helped Joel recognize and clarify the overall impact of the changes he had made.]

Discussion. Without directly challenging or discounting Joel's feelings of depression and hopelessness, the formula first session task invited him to look at his life through a lens that focused on what *was* working instead of what was not working. Although not all students respond as positively as Joel did, this simple exception-finding task works well with most people and most problems.

The method of utilizing exceptions, or working with what works, is conceptually simple and pragmatic: find something that works and have people do more of it. However, putting this into practice can be very challenging because it requires a major shift in the way that practitioners have typically approached school behavior problems and the people who experience them.

SUMMARY AND CONCLUSIONS

1. Based on the premise that it is easier to move something in the direction that it is already going, the strategy of utilizing exceptions capitalizes on aspects of the problem situation that are already moving in the direction of a solution.

2. The 5-E Method, a systematic process of utilizing exceptions to school problems, is composed of five interrelated steps:

- *Eliciting* an exception to the problem
- *Elaborating* the details and circumstances associated with the exception
- *Expanding* the exception to other situations and to a greater frequency
- *Evaluating* the effectiveness of intervention
- *Empowering* and maintaining desired changes

3. The utilization of exceptions to resolve school problems was illustrated by case examples involving a middle school student who demonstrated behavior problems ("The Exceptional Quarter"), a group counseling intervention for test-anxious students ("The Competent Test-Anxiety Group"), and a high school student who complained of depression ("The Student for Whom Nothing Was Going Right").

Utilizing exceptions is based on the first intervention guideline of solution-focused counseling: If it works, do more of it. The utility of this guideline is further illustrated in the next chapter.

PRACTICE EXERCISES

1. Think of a problem you are currently struggling with. Now think about times or circumstances in which the problem is less noticeable or troublesome. Ask yourself the following questions:

   - What is different about those times?
   - What am I doing differently in these situations in the way I approach, think about, and respond to the situation or people involved in it?
   - What can I do to make this happen more often or in other situations?

2. When discussing a school problem during your next counseling session, ask the client to describe times when the problem doesn't happen or when it is less noticeable.

3. When you meet with students, parents, or teachers for the first time, ask if they have noticed any slight changes or improvements in the problem since scheduling the meeting. If they indicate that such changes have occurred, explore the details of these exceptions.

4. Incorporate at least one or more of the following interviewing strategies in your next meeting with a student, parent, or teacher:

- scaling questions
- miracle questions
- exception-finding questions

5. During the next week, write a note to a student, parent, or teacher complimenting them on something they have accomplished in relation to a school problem they are dealing with. Observe their reactions to the note.
6. Have your partner report desired changes in a problem, and practice the strategy of blaming the client by using questions and comments that attribute such changes to the client.

Utilizing Other Client Resources

We awaken in others the same attitude of mind we hold toward them.

—Elbert Hubbard

Solution-focused counseling is based on the assumption that students, parents, and teachers have the resources to change school problems. Instead of focusing strictly on what people need to have or need to do in order to change, this approach utilizes what they already have and are already doing. Building on exceptions to the problem is one way to tap what students and others are already doing to contribute to solutions. This chapter provides strategies for utilizing other resources that clients bring to counseling.

Client resources that can be applied toward resolving school problems include the following:

- *Special talents, interests, and hobbies* (sports, movies, television shows, music, singing, being a good listener, mechanical activities, bicycling, and so forth)
- *Heroes* (parents, siblings, friends, actors, athletes, musicians, and any other real or fictional persons that represent heroes for the client)
- *Resilience and coping skills* (abilities to withstand and cope with various difficulties in life, including the school problem)
- *Social supports* (family, friends, co-workers, house of worship, social service agencies, and so forth)
- *Ideas for resolving the school problem* (the client's own ideas regarding potential solutions)

THE PROCESS OF UTILIZING CLIENT RESOURCES

The process of utilizing other client resources closely resembles the process of utilizing exceptions. Resources, like exceptions, are identified, clarified, and applied to the school problem.

Identifying, Clarifying, and Applying Client Resources

Listen. People often reveal potentially useful resources in the course of conversation regarding a school problem. I recall the case of a middle school student who was referred for counseling due to classroom misbehavior. Behavior problems were especially noticeable during the two classes following lunch. In the midst of discussing the problem, he commented that he would do much better in school if he were allowed to play baseball for a few minutes between classes. We spent several minutes discussing his love of baseball. I asked him how baseball and school were alike, and we began discussing similarities between the challenges of school and the challenges of baseball. We talked about how long a baseball season is, and how important it is to not let a few bad games ruin the entire season. The student agreed to try a baseball approach to his classes, which involved increased efforts on his part to "step up to the plate every day" and do his best, even though he would inevitably "strike out" sometimes. He came back in 2 weeks and told me that things were better, and that he had shared the baseball metaphor with a friend who also got into a lot of trouble at school.

Ask. Most people do not spontaneously volunteer information about their hobbies, interests, heroes, and other resources. Therefore, it is usually necessary to directly ask about these. Questions for discovering and clarifying client resources include the following:

- What kinds of things do you enjoy doing outside of school?
- What would your friends say that you are good at if I asked them?
- Who is one of your heroes?
- Of all the people in your life, who helps you the most?
- What does that person do or say that really helps you?

Look. Practitioners can look for resources in school records or other documents. School records sometimes include information about a student's special interests and talents. For example, vocational interest inventories and teachers' comments on report cards can be useful in identifying potential resources.

Apply. Utilizing client resources illustrates the solution-focused strategy of including as much of the client as possible in interventions for school problems. In the case of the student who loved baseball, *he* supplied the core material for intervention, not me. Once a potentially useful resource is identified, our task is to help people apply it to the problem. The remainder of this chapter illustrates how this can be done with a variety of school problems.

CASE EXAMPLES OF UTILIZING CLIENT RESOURCES

The following cases show how client resources can be utilized in various practical ways in school counseling. As illustrated by these examples, capitalizing on what people bring to counseling is a cooperative way to create solutions.

Dorothy's Advice

Bridgette was referred by several ninth-grade teachers for "mouthing off" during class and completing only half of her school assignments. The teachers reported that she was capable of doing adequate work, but that she only applied herself when she felt like it. Bridgette was suspended for 3 days during the previous month, and was very close to being suspended again when I met with her. She had attended several different elementary schools, and experienced discipline problems at each one of them. Most previous attempts to address the situation involved efforts to find out why she was misbehaving and attempts to reason with her about the connection between her behavior and negative consequences such as suspension.

Within the opening minutes of the first interview, Bridgette commented that she "hated school" and was "tired of schoolwork." I dropped the subject of school and asked about her hobbies. She said she loved watching old movies with her mother on Sunday afternoons. Her favorite movie was *The Wizard of Oz*. I told her that this was one of my favorites as well, and asked her what she liked best about it. Bridgette named several parts of the movie that she particularly liked. She commented that Dorothy, the main character, "always looked ahead at how things would be better" instead of "moping around" about being away from home. She added that Dorothy "didn't let anything stop her." Here's what happened next.

Counselor: Do you ever feel like Dorothy, with all these problems happening at school?

Bridgette: All the time. [*laughs*]

Counselor: You get over one problem in one class, and then something else happens in another class to set you back.

Bridgette: Exactly.

Counselor: This might seem like a weird question, but how do you think Dorothy would handle this school stuff that you're dealing with?

Bridgette: I don't know. I guess she would say "don't let it get you down," or something like that.

Counselor: What other words or advice would Dorothy have for you?

Bridgette: She would say, "don't let them get you down or stop you."

Counselor: Stop you from what?

Bridgette: From getting through school, I guess.

Counselor: Do you want to get through school?

Bridgette: Yes.

Counselor: Why? What's so important about getting through school?

Bridgette: Graduating, because if you don't graduate you'll end up on the street. You don't have any money, no job, stuff like that. Who would want that?

Counselor: Well, some people don't seem to care whether or not they graduate. But you're saying that you do, right?

Bridgette: Yes. I want to graduate and get a decent job so I can have a decent life.

Counselor: So Dorothy would say "don't let anybody or anything stop you from your goal of graduating," huh?

Bridgette: Yes. She didn't let anything stop her. She just kept going.

Counselor: What are some things you could do to follow Dorothy's advice about not letting anything stop you from graduating?

Bridgette: Well, I guess I could shut up more in class.

Counselor: I'll bet that's going to be really hard. Especially since you're used to doing it a lot.

Bridgette: Yeah, it will be hard. Especially in some classes.

The conversation proceeded to clarify specific ways that Bridgette could apply "Dorothy's advice" to school, including asking her mother for help with difficult homework, and sitting closer to the front of the room in a couple of her classes. We talked about how difficult it would be to approach a teacher to ask if she could sit closer to the front of the classroom. Bridgette wanted to be viewed as "independent and tough." Toughness and self-reliance were very much a part of Bridgette's familial and cultural environment. I attempted to honor and accommodate her views by suggesting that "perhaps it is actually 'tougher' to have the courage to try and change something than to 'wimp out' and expect others to change things for you." Bridgette agreed to approach one or two of her teachers to request a seating change. Before the session ended, we role-played a couple of situations in which Bridgette approached the teacher (me) and asked if she could sit closer to the front of the room.

Bridgette implemented Dorothy's advice, and her school performance progressed steadily over the next few months. School attendance improved by about 60 percent during the following 2 months. Bridgette was not suspended during those 2 months, and received only 4 days of after-school detention as compared to 13 days of detention during the 2 months prior to our meeting. She also brought her grades up in two classes, from F to D in one class and from D to B in another.

Discussion. Bridgette had already heard all the standard reasons why she should change. Her teachers predicted that she would not be very cooperative, and Bridgette herself appeared to enter the session expecting to hear the same old lectures. A different approach was clearly warranted. Exploring and utilizing Bridgette's resources was useful in building cooperation and conveying the notion that this counseling experience was going to be very different than previous attempts to address the problem. If I had *told* her to change her behavior, or to approach her teachers about sitting closer to the front of the room, it is doubtful that she would have cooperated. When it comes to middle and high school students, a common rule of cooperation is, "you've got to give it to get it." This case also demonstrates how other established intervention strategies such as role-playing and behavioral rehearsal (Cormier & Cormier, 1991) can be used in ways that fit the client's goals and positions.

Bridgette's case illustrates how solutions can evolve from resources that appear very remote from the school problem. These resources may never be discovered unless we listen and ask for them. Paying attention to client resources opens up solution possibilities that would otherwise remain hidden and untapped. After all, "Wizard of Oz Interventions" are not typically covered in graduate training programs.

Sweeping the Sidewalk Twice

The counselor in this case was Michael Walters of Boone County (Kentucky) Public Schools. Roy was an eighth grader referred by the school principal and his parents for failing grades, refusing to complete school work, cursing, and arguing with teachers. Roy's mother informed the counselor that she and her husband had very little control of him at home. When asked about what Roy did well, his mother said that he worked hard at his lawn mowing job and managed his money pretty well.

During the opening minutes of the first interview, Roy stated that he "hated" school, homework, and most of his teachers (especially Ms. Cahill, his math teacher). The counselor shifted the conversation to client resources as follows.

Counselor: Your mother says you work really hard mowing lawns, and that you've made some money at it.

Roy: Yes.

Counselor: What's the same about school and this job?

Roy: They're not the same. You get paid for mowing.

Counselor: What do you have to do to get paid?

Roy: You have to do the job.

Counselor: Do you do the job?

Roy: Yes. One time Mr. Kruger only paid us half. He said we didn't sweep the sidewalk.

Counselor: Do you still mow his grass?

Roy: Yes, and we sweep the walk twice now.

Counselor: Do any of your teachers remind you of Mr. Kruger?

Roy: Ms. Cahill (math teacher). If you do one little thing wrong, she's on your case.

Counselor: What do you do to help save your money?

Roy: Keep track of it. I know how much I make and I know how much I can spend. I'm saving to buy a four-wheeler.

Counselor: How well do you keep track of your school work?
Roy: Not very well. I don't get paid for that.

The counselor continued to draw analogies between mowing grass and doing school work. The report card was compared to a paycheck, a crabby lawn mowing customer to a crabby teacher, and keeping track of money to keeping track of school work. The counselor also clarified Roy's success at his lawn mowing job by asking him how he managed to hold the job and keep at it when things got tough.

Roy stated that he wanted to pass school, and he and the counselor developed a small, specific goal for passing the eighth grade. Roy calculated exactly how many points he needed to get a D in the two classes he was failing.

The counselor suggested that Roy approach his goal of passing all classes the same way he approaches his lawn mowing job. Using Roy's language, the intervention plan was to "do the job" and "sweep Ms. Cahill's sidewalk twice." This basically translated to studying for tests or not arguing with teachers in class. When they met a week later, Roy reported improved school performance and no discipline referrals. In an effort to empower Roy's success, the counselor asked, "How did you do that?" A person of few words, Roy simply said, "I just did the job like we talked about."

In addition to favorable comments from several of his teachers, Roy's academic and behavioral improvements were verified by his teachers and his grades. First and second quarter grades were compared to evaluate the effectiveness of intervention. Roy's first quarter report card included one C, one D, and four F's. His second quarter grades improved markedly in the form of two A's, one B, two C's, and one F. The F was in Ms. Cahill's math class. However, Ms. Cahill reported no further discipline problems with Roy, and he passed to the ninth grade.

Discussion. This case illustrates how a student's competence and attitudes in a nonschool area of life can be effectively applied to a school problem. Roy's lawn mowing experience provided a useful metaphor and set of skills that were applicable to the problems he was facing in school. The counselor's alertness to other client resources outside of the school setting led to an intervention that accommodated Roy's unique position, goals, and talents, and that was very different than previous ineffective attempts to force him into compliance.

Consulting Camus

Dwayne, an intellectually gifted 12th grader, was referred in early March because he had failed to complete some assignments that were required for graduation. There were no doubts whatsoever regarding his ability to do the work, and the teachers felt as if they had exhausted all attempts to reason with Dwayne about the importance of the required work. The teachers and administrative staff were extremely concerned, as was Dwayne's mother, who thought that Dwayne might need to be referred to a psychiatrist to "find out what was going on with him."

The major theme of previous solution attempts was to convince Dwayne that all he had to do was turn in a few required papers to graduate, even if the quality was mediocre. Because this approach had not worked, a different approach was warranted. The following dialogue occurred in the opening moments of the first interview with Dwayne.

Counselor: It would help me to ask you a few quick questions to get a better handle on this thing. You know a lot more about this than I do, so I need your help in filling me in on what's going on with this graduation thing, and required papers, and so forth. Okay?

Dwayne: Okay.

Counselor: Thanks. First off, do you want to graduate, or is this just something everybody else thinks you should do?

Dwayne: I definitely want to graduate.

Counselor: Why?

Dwayne: I want to go to college.

Counselor: And graduation is the ticket to college, right?

Dwayne: Right.

Counselor: Okay. Thanks. That helps me, because before we start talking about stuff, I want to make sure I know what *you* want out of this whole thing. So, exactly what do you need to do in order to graduate?

Dwayne: There are some required papers. It's not required that you get good grades, just that you turn them in. They're all overdue. The most important one is the 4,000 word essay. My essay is on comparing Camus' *The Stranger* to Hemingway's *The Old Man and the Sea*. I've got an A in that course. I've just got to write it and turn it in. [*During the next few minutes, Dwayne shared the idea that he did not want to "just turn it in" for the sake of the grade.*]

Counselor: Do you think that once you get into this stuff and you get to know these ideas so well, that it's sort of ridiculous to have to write them up for someone else?

Dwayne: Exactly. I made a mistake to write about Camus because he's my personal hero. I like existentialism.

[*As he discussed the writings of philosopher/author Albert Camus, it became obvious that Dwayne had a tremendous knowledge and respect for him. Next, Dwayne discusses the essay paper that had been the focal point of teacher concerns.*]

Dwayne: I've got plenty of notes on the essay right now.

Counselor: Interesting. And yet you haven't written it.

[*Next, the counselor explores the possibility of a connection between Dwayne's choice to not complete the essay and his respect for Camus and existentialism. The counselor offers this possibility in the form of a "dilemma".*]

Counselor: I can appreciate the dilemma you have about Camus in that it's easier to write about something you don't care that much about or don't know much about.

Dwayne: That's it. I wouldn't want to cut out things that I thought were important if it came to that, because he's one of my personal heroes.

Counselor: Yeah.

Dwayne: The counselors told me that I'm too perfectionistic. I *want* to do it perfectly. I don't want to turn in something that's not good. I know it just has to be there for me to get credit. It doesn't have to make sense. It just has to be 4,000 words.

Counselor: Now, this question might sound bizarre. Do you actually dialogue with Camus in your own head? Have you had dynamic conversations with Camus, imagining what you would say and what he would say?

Dwayne: Lots of times.

Counselor: Maybe this whole paper issue would be something you could talk with him about and see what emerges. See what kind of feedback he might give you with this dilemma. It seems to me that you would respect his opinion more than anybody else's right now.

Dwayne: [*laughs, nods head "yes"*]

[*Clients usually provide various nonverbal indicators of their acceptance or rejection of an idea including head nods, raised eyebrows, leaning forward in the chair, looking pensive, and so forth. Dwayne's verbal and nonverbal response to this suggestion was very positive, and the counselor continued to explore it with him.*]

Counselor: You've already had some experience in dialoguing with Camus. What do you think he might say?

Dwayne: Hmmm [*pauses for several seconds*]. I think he'd say do it, and that it doesn't have to be a masterpiece.

Counselor: So he would understand your dilemma?

Dwayne: Yes. Camus always talked about how there's a need for discipline in life, but there's also a need to break off from discipline at times. I guess this would be a time to have discipline in my life.

Counselor: Interesting. So he would be okay with you not including everything you know about him, as long as you did it for discipline's sake?

Dwayne: Yes. Especially when you weigh all the possible benefits I could get out of it compared to the discomfort it would cause if I didn't do it.

Counselor: Is he pretty pragmatic about some of those benefits?

Dwayne: Yes.

Counselor: What other advice do you think Camus would offer about this dilemma you're facing?

Dwayne: Just do it.

Counselor: Interesting.

The session ended with the counselor encouraging Dwayne to consider other advice that Camus would offer, and to decide what he wanted to do with such advice. In order not to duplicate the theme and pattern of previous interventions, the counselor made no mention of doing anything regarding the 4,000-word essay or other assignments. Dwayne completed the essay within 3 weeks, although he waited on some of the other assignments until a week or so before graduation. The counselor sent Dwayne a letter and award to recognize his completion of graduation requirements (see Exhibits 7.1 and 7.2).

Exhibit 7.1. Congratulatory Letter to Dwayne

Dear Dwayne:

I want to congratulate you on your recent completion of several key tasks associated with completing your school program in order to graduate. I know how difficult this was, and I am impressed with the discipline you showed in dealing with this dilemma. I suspect that Camus would be pleased with the practical strategy you adopted to bite the bullet and "just do it" in order to move on to other life adventures.

Please accept the enclosed Bite the Bullet Award as recognition of your "existential" accomplishment. Best wishes in the journey ahead.

Sincerely,

JM

Exhibit 7.2. "Bite the Bullet" Award for Dwayne

The Bite the Bullet Award

This is to recognize the existential accomplishment of

Dwayne M.

for a pragmatic display of discipline in "biting the bullet" and completing the assignments required for graduation.

Discussion. The parents' and teachers' previous efforts to reason with Dwayne lacked sufficient meaning for him, because they did not connect to a dilemma that was much more significant to him than getting credit—the dilemma of how to summarize the ideas of Camus, his personal hero, in a way that did them justice. The perspectives and suggestions of Camus, a most important resource in Dwayne's life, provided an avenue to a solution in this case.

"Success Stories": A Schoolwide Program for Recognizing Resilience and Resources

This case study describes a program aimed at recognizing, clarifying, and empowering the successes and resources of middle school students. Videotaped interviews were conducted with students who made major academic or behavioral improvements during the school year, and their responses were included in a movie entitled *Success Stories*.

The Success Stories program was initiated for the following purposes: (a) to formally recognize specific school improvements in order to help students clarify and maintain them; (b) to provide a permanent product and source of ideas (a videotape) for improving school performance for future use by school staff, parents, and students; (c) to provide a morale boost for school staff by focusing on successful students; and (d) to implement a schoolwide application of utilizing students as consultants.

In early May, a note was sent to every teacher explaining the purposes of the project and requesting the names of two students who had successfully improved their academic work or behavior over the course of the year, even if it was only in one particular subject area or one aspect of behavior. Each student was interviewed individually on videotape regarding his or her success. Interviews lasted about 10 minutes, and students were asked variations of the following questions:

- How did you improve your grades/behavior at school this year?
- How are things different for you at home and school since you have made these improvements?
- What helped you hang in there this year when things got tough?
- If other students asked you to help them improve their grades/behavior, what would you tell them?

These questions highlight the solution-focused emphasis on resilience and resources. The following excerpt is taken from a portion of an interview with a sixth-grade student named Larita, who raised her grades from an average of D the first semester to B the second semester. The dialogue begins with some questions about how these positive changes have affected different areas of Larita's life.

Interviewer: Do the teachers treat you any differently now with better grades than they did when your grades were lower?

Larita: Yes. Better.

Interviewer: How?

Larita: When I had bad grades, they really didn't help me because I really didn't want to do the work, but now they're starting to help me.

Interviewer: So the more they see that you want to do the work, the more willing they are to spend the time to help you?

Larita: Yes.

Interviewer: Okay. Are there any other changes in the way that you're treated, either at home or school, now that your grades are better?

Larita: I used to get a lot of detentions, but now that I'm not hanging around my old friends, I haven't gotten a lot of detentions.

Interviewer: Do your old friends still try to get you to hang around with them?

Larita: Yes.

Interviewer: I imagine it's hard to resist the temptation. Probably hard to say no sometimes, isn't it?

Larita: Yes.

Interviewer: How do you manage to do that?

Larita: I just walk away.

Interviewer: What advice would you give other students to help them improve their schoolwork?

Larita: Volunteer more. Answer questions in class.

Interviewer: What other tips would you give them?

Larita: Don't try be a teacher's pet, because it will probably annoy them.

Discussion. Although definitive conclusions about the benefits of this experience for students cannot be made, several students commented that the interview helped them to better understand how they improved in school. The videotape remains on file at the school to be reviewed by school staff, parents, and other students as a source of ideas for improving grades and behavior. The Success Stories program was practical in the sense of being inexpensive and requiring very little teacher time. These are important considerations for any school program.

SUMMARY AND CONCLUSIONS

1. Every person brings unique resources to the counseling process in the form of special interests, talents, ideas, and social supports. Counselors can discover these resources by listening, asking, and looking for them in their work with students, teachers, and parents.

2. Once a resource is discovered and clarified, counselors can help clients apply it to the school problem at hand.

3. The strategy of applying unique client resources was illustrated by case examples of a ninth grader who demonstrated behavioral and academic difficulties ("Dorothy's Advice"), an eighth-grade student who argued and cursed at teachers ("Sweeping the Sidewalk Twice"), a high school senior who was in jeopardy of not graduating ("Consulting Camus"), and a schoolwide program to recognize students' resilience and resources ("Success Stories").

As illustrated by the cases in this chapter, resources come in all shapes and sizes, and from various aspects of a person's life. I am continually amazed at how something that seems so remote from the school problem can be effectively applied toward its solution.

PRACTICE EXERCISES

1. Select a difficulty you are currently experiencing. Now think of a specific difficulty or challenge that you have successfully overcome or coped with in your own life. How did you manage to do this? What type of attitudes, beliefs, and actions contributed to your success in this situation? How could these attitudes, beliefs, and actions be adapted and applied to your current difficulty? Ask some of your clients these types of questions in order to help them consider how their successes and skills in handling challenges in other areas of their lives might be applied to their current school problem.

2. If asked about your special skills and talents, what would your friends and colleagues say? What would you say? How can these talents and skills be utilized in your work as a counselor?

3. Pick one or two clients during the next week, and ask about their special hobbies, interests, and talents. Consider how these resources might be applied to the school problem.

Changing the Doing of the Problem

If at first you don't succeed, try again. Then quit. There's no use being a damn fool about it.

—W. C. Fields

Encouraging people to apply what works is a practical and cooperative way to bring about solutions based on the intervention guideline, "if it works, do more of it." These strategies typically are attempted first because they utilize the successes and resources that are already part of the natural repertoire of students, parents, and teachers. In some situations, however, other strategies are required. People may not provide exceptions to the problem, or they may express a preference for a different type of intervention.

This is the first of two chapters based on the second guideline of solution-focused counseling: *If it doesn't work, try something different.* The MRI model (Watzlawick et al., 1974) suggests that people's attempted solutions become part of the problem. Consider the example of a student who skips school in response to what she perceives as unrealistic parental demands. This prompts more of the same demands from the parents, and the student responds by skipping even more. People often become entrenched in such cycles because they believe that whatever it is that they are doing is the only right and sensible response or solution to the problem (Fisch et al., 1982; Watzlawick et al., 1974). In these cases, the problem will continue indefinitely until something noticeably different occurs in place of the usual interpretations ("viewing") or actions ("doing") that accompany it. Therefore, intervention seeks to block or interrupt these repetitive patterns in order to allow for different responses to the problem.

The strategies presented in these two chapters encourage changes in the way students and others do and view the problem. Because changing the doing and viewing of problems is the aim of many counseling approaches, these chapters cover strategies that are rather unique to the solution-focused approach and to the literature on school counseling. In practice, "doing" and "viewing" interventions are frequently used in conjunction with one another in dealing with a school problem. However, these two intervention strategies are addressed separately in this book for the sake of clarity. Chapter 9 deals with changing the viewing, whereas this chapter addresses changing the doing of school problems. Before describing specific interventions for interrupting ineffective solution attempts by doing something different, some common strategies that typically fail to change middle and high school problems are presented.

SOLUTION ATTEMPTS THAT USUALLY FAIL

The following methods of addressing adolescents' school problems are frequently employed by teachers, parents, and professionals. There is nothing inherently wrong with these strategies. In fact, they may work well with some students in some circumstances. However, when unsuccessfully applied and reapplied to a school problem, they make things worse instead of better. Parts of the following discussion are adapted from Cade and O'Hanlon (1993) and Fisch et al. (1982) where indicated.

Logical Reasoning

This strategy assumes that students will change once they realize how illogical their position is, and how sensible the parent's, teacher's, or counselor's position is. Airtight and unassailable logic may work wonders in the courtroom, but it bombs with adolescents who are not buying what adults are trying to sell.

Unsolicited Lectures and Advice
(Adapted From Cade & O'Hanlon, 1993)

This strategy typically takes the form of a parent, teacher, or counselor providing unsolicited advice and lectures to the student. Common lecture themes include the following:

- the value of an education
- the observation that students are only hurting themselves
- Statistics regarding the dangers of [dropping out, smoking, not getting a degree, etc.]. This can be done directly in face-to-face discussions, or indirectly by placing pertinent brochures, pamphlets, or magazine articles in strategic locations such as the kitchen countertop or the student's book bag.

Guilt Trips

These solution attempts can be presented to students in one of the following ways:

- Can't you see what you're doing to [me, your mother, our family, our reputation]?
- I'll love you even more if you [start making better grades, mind the teachers, quit skipping school].
- If you really loved me, then you would stop doing this.
- After all I've done to try and help you do better in school, this is what I get in return. [A more desperate version of this might include reference to the number of times the parent has cared for the student when she or he was sick, drove the student places, changed diapers, etc.]

Denial, Avoidance, Protection, and Responsibility (Adapted From Cade & O'Hanlon, 1993)

This set of strategies is usually displayed by parents in one of the following ways:

- Claiming that all of the student's problems result solely from an adolescent stage ("It's just a phase").
- Walking on eggshells and otherwise avoiding the subject of the school problem at all costs.
- Protecting students from the natural consequences of their actions by frequently criticizing the school or teachers, intervening with the school board, and otherwise attempting to "help" the student.
- Taking on progressively more responsibility for the school problem while trying to get the student to become more responsible; doing more and more as the student does less and less.

Forcing Something That Can Only Happen Spontaneously (Adapted From Fisch et al., 1982)

This strategy seeks to force or talk students into desires, attitudes, and other "spontaneous" responses. Examples include:

- Attempting to persuade the student to feel more responsible, compassionate, motivated, etc.
- Implying that students not only *need* to change, but *want* to change; suggesting that change is somehow better and more authentic when students want to change rather than changing just because parents or teachers want them to.

Winning Versus Doing What Works

Teachers and parents may assume this position when they feel that they are being manipulated by the student into changing their approach. Changing is viewed as giving in or losing, while standing one's ground and not changing is viewed as winning. This position is captured by the following thoughts and statements on the part of teachers and parents:

- I'll show this student who's in charge. I'm not budging.
- Why should *I* be the one to change when it is *his* or *her* problem?

Escalating Punishments

This category includes strategies in which progressively stronger punishments are administered despite their ineffectiveness in altering the problem. Escalating punishments often result in escalating problems. This strategy may be fueled by the win–lose position discussed above, or by the notion that the original punishment was not strong enough, and more of it will help to improve things.

Probing Underlying Reasons or Causes

This strategy is employed by counselors, parents, and teachers, and usually takes on variations of the question, "What's *really* going on with you to cause you to do this?" Many adolescents are guarded and cautious in their self-disclosure with adults, especially when they perceive the adult's questioning as a search for pathology or an infringement on their privacy.

This section was provided to help school practitioners recognize ineffective attempts to resolve middle and high school problems. Because these strategies are typically implemented with the sincere intention to help students, it is important not to blame or criticize parents and teachers for these ineffective methods.

INTERRUPTING THE PROBLEM BY CHANGING THE DOING

Interventions presented in this chapter seek to interrupt the problem pattern by encouraging people to do something different in their usual performance of the problem itself, or in their responses to the problem. There are an unlimited number of interventions from the literature that may be useful in interrupting school problems by altering the actions of a student, teacher, or parent. The literature suggests that some interventions are very effective for certain types of problems. In dealing with children's anxiety problems, for example, cognitive-behavioral coping strategies have been shown to be very effective (Barrios & O'Dell, 1989; Kronenberger & Meyer, 1996). However, any type of intervention must be tailored to fit the unique style and circumstances of the client if it is to be effective. Counseling theories typically include a set of intervention strategies based on the content of the theory. For example, behavioral theory advocates the use of reinforcement methods to alter problems, whereas psychodynamic approaches emphasize the role of unconscious processes and self-exploration.

As useful as one particular theory or set of strategies may be with some clients and some problems, no one theory or technique works all the time with every person and every problem. Solution-focused counseling draws from a variety of theories and techniques to select interventions. However, this chapter focuses only on those strategies that are somewhat unique to the solution-focused approach and to the school counseling literature.

SPECIFIC INTERVENTIONS FOR CHANGING THE DOING

The following list, adapted from O'Hanlon (1987, pp. 36–37), presents several practical ways that students, parents, and teachers can be encouraged to "change the doing" of school problems. A short school-related example is provided for each intervention.

1. *Changing the frequency of the problem/problem pattern.* In a situation where the parents remind a student about homework completion several times a day, encourage them to alter the frequency of reminders to six randomly selected times per week.

2. *Changing the duration of the problem/problem pattern.* For a student who frequently argues with her teachers, suggest an experiment in which she changes the length of "argument time" and observes the effects of different durations on the extent to which the teachers hassle her.

3. *Changing the time of day/week/month of the problem/problem pattern.* In a situation where the teacher and student often argue about missing assignments when the student arrives to class each day, suggest that they schedule one argument per week on Wednesday afternoons immediately after school.

4. *Changing the location of the problem/problem pattern.* In the case when the problem behavior typically occurs in the classroom, encourage the student to "do the problem" in the lunchroom instead.

5. *Changing the intensity of the problem/problem pattern.* If the teacher typically reprimands the student in a loud voice, encourage the teacher to whisper reprimands to the student.

6. *Changing some other quality or circumstance of the problem/problem pattern.* In a circumstance where the parents and the student engage in verbal battles regarding the student's school performance, suggest to the father that he do something different with his voice or language during the next few school-related conversations as a way of "shaking things up a bit."

7. *Changing the sequence or order of events in the problem pattern.* In a situation where the teacher typically confronts the student about classroom misbehavior, and the student ends up saying "I'm sorry, I'll try to do better," encourage the student to apologize upon arriving to class each day in order to "get it over with."

8. *Interrupting or otherwise preventing all or part of the problem sequence from occurring ("derailing").* In the case of repetitive conflicts between the student and his mother, encourage the parent to say "Wait a minute, I'll be right back," upon the first sign of an argument, then walk out the door and work in the yard, take the dog for a walk, or so forth.

9. *Adding or subtracting (at least) one element to or from the sequence.* For a student who rarely does homework, encourage the student to turn in "something" for every homework assignment, if only a piece of paper with his or her name on it.

10. *Breaking up any element of the problem into smaller elements.* In the case of a middle school teacher who has to constantly remind the student to bring his notebook, pencil, book, and other required materials to class each day, encourage the teacher to walk up to the student, kneel down at eye level, and painstakingly review *every* single item that he should bring to class (perhaps even discussing the specific qualities or "history" of items such as the pencil, eraser, etc.).

11. *Performing the problem without the problem pattern.* For a student who frequently daydreams in class, suggest that the student practice daydreaming while in her living room at home or while riding in a car.

12. *Reversing the pattern.* In the case of parent–adolescent conflict in which discussions often end with the student stomping out of the room and claiming that his parents "just don't understand," suggest that the student stomp out of the room first, then re-enter the room and proceed with comments that typically occur right before he stomps out of the room.

13. *Linking the occurrence of the problem to another undesirable or avoided activity (creating an ordeal).* In a situation where the student expresses a strong desire to attend school more regularly along with self-doubts regarding her ability to do so, recommend an ordeal in which she agrees to wash a load of laundry for each day she misses school.

14. *Adding an element of surprise or confusion to the problem pattern.* When the student is highly critical or argumentative on a regular basis, encourage the teacher or parent to comment on the student's dress or voice qualities instead of the content of his or her statements, or to respond as if something entirely different had been said.

15. *Observing instead of acting on the problem.* In a situation where parents unsuccessfully but persistently try to talk their daughter out of feeling depressed, suggest that they observe her for a week without talking to her in order to identify the times that she appears least depressed and to obtain a more thorough assessment of the situation.

The strategies listed above are not typical school interventions, which is precisely their strength. By the time teachers or parents make a counseling referral, they have usually made reasonable attempts to resolve the problem. Some middle and high school problems that land on the counselor's desk have persisted for months or even years in the face of various reasonable or conventional intervention strategies. Something very different is required in these cases.

This chapter encourages counselors to "sing a different song" instead of becoming one more voice in the "more of the same" chorus. The 15 intervention strategies listed above are but a few of the many possible ways to help people change the doing of school problems. Changing the doing can take on as many forms as the counselor's and client's creativity allows. The challenge of counseling does not stem from a lack of techniques, but from the task of designing interventions to fit the unique goals, positions, and circumstances of the client.

THE "DO SOMETHING DIFFERENT" TASK

In cases when the counselor's mind goes blank, or when no particular intervention appears to fit the client's situation, counselors can suggest the "do something different" task by (a) acknowledging that something different is required, but that it is unclear exactly what that could be; and (b) encouraging the client to do something different in response to the problem during the coming week, and to pay attention to any changes that result from it.

I recall the case of Keisha, an eighth grader referred by her parents for cursing and yelling at them. I met with both parents during the first session because they were the most obvious customers for change. I suggested that one or both of them try doing something different the next time Keisha cursed at them. In the past, the parents typically sent Keisha to her room and removed car privileges after such incidents. These methods did not help to decrease her arguing and cursing.

I met with the parents 1 week later and asked if they had tried anything different. They looked at each other and smiled. Keisha's mother explained that they decided to "stage" an argument in order to better understand the dynamics of their relationship with Keisha (the mother was a counselor). They calmly explained this to Keisha, informing her that one of them would observe and take notes while the other was engaged in an argument with her. The arguments and cursing subsided following this strategy. As illustrated in this case, clients often develop creative strategies in response to the do something different task.

CASE EXAMPLES OF CHANGING THE DOING

The following cases illustrate the process of "changing the doing" of school problems to bring about solutions.

The Lovesick Senior

Bruce, an 18-year-old student in his senior year of high school, was referred by his math teacher due to a sudden change in behavior and attitude. During the week preceding the referral, Bruce appeared to be very agitated. He left class twice without permission, and spoke very harshly to the teacher and other students. According to his teacher, these behaviors were very uncharacteristic of Bruce, who typically displayed a calm demeanor and spoke politely to both teachers and students.

The counselor began the first meeting with Bruce by asking if he knew why his teacher requested counseling for him. Bruce replied that he had been "feeling and acting strange," and that he understood why the teacher asked him to talk to a counselor. He explained that he had recently broken up with his girlfriend, whom he had gone with for 2 years. He added that he had been getting about 2 hours of sleep per night since the breakup, and that he "could not stop thinking about it." He looked very distraught and fatigued.

The counselor asked Bruce what he viewed as the most important problem or issue, the breakup itself or worrying and thinking about it. Bruce said that the relationship was definitely over, and that his biggest concern was "not being able to get it out of my head." When he thought about the breakup, he would immediately try to think of something else. This strategy did not help. Bruce's best friend urged him to "just get over it," and his mother attempted to console him by reminding him that "there are plenty of fish in the sea." He said that he understood what they meant and knew that they were right, yet he just could not shake it from his mind. He stated that he thought about it all the time at school, at home, and while working at his restaurant job. Bruce's description suggested a problem pattern in which the harder he tried not to think about it, the more he thought about it. When asked if it helped to think about it, Bruce said it helped a little because it provided some insight into the breakup. The following dialogue ensued.

Counselor: I don't know how anybody could stop thinking about something that's so important in their lives as this is for you. I'm also not sure it's a good idea to stop thinking about it, since it may help you to figure out some things about the relationship. You know, where things went wrong and stuff like that. In fact, thinking about it might not be what's keeping you up at night. It might be that you're not giving it the proper focus and attention it deserves.
Bruce: [looking puzzled] What do you mean?
Counselor: Well, I'm just wondering whether you can do it justice by trying to think about it in the midst of distractions at school and work. How can you properly clear your head and really think clearly about it if the teacher's talking to you about school stuff, or your boss is telling you to do something at work?

[The counselor's comment is in direct contrast to Bruce's prevailing solution attempt of "trying to forget about it," and also is very different than his mother's and friend's advice to "forget about it." Next, the counselor continues to acknowledge and match Bruce's position regarding the importance of the breakup while exploring different ways to "do justice" to the issue.]

Bruce: It's hard to think about anything at work.

Counselor: Would you say your performance at work and school has been better, worse, or about the same since you broke up?

Bruce: A lot worse.

Counselor: A lot worse. So, not only is it hard to think clearly about the breakup, but school and work and sleep are not going as well for you.

Bruce: Right.

Counselor: What time of day would it be the easiest for you to really concentrate on this and give it some thought instead of trying to do it at school and work? You know, a 15 or 20 minute period where you might really be able to focus and perhaps figure something out.

Bruce: I guess after dinner.

Counselor: Would you be willing to try an experiment where you would pick a few days during the coming week to use that time to really focus in and think about the breakup?

Bruce: Yes.

Counselor: Which days do you want to try it?

Bruce's primary solution attempt, "trying real hard not to think about it," actually intensified the problem instead of relieving it. If implemented, the counselor's suggestion to think about it would disallow Bruce's solution attempt, interrupt the existing problem pattern, and perhaps allow for a more productive response to the situation. Bruce decided to schedule 20 minutes of "think time" every other evening.

Bruce returned for the second counseling session looking considerably more energetic than he did the week before. When asked how his week went, he said that it was much better and that he did not worry nearly as much as he had. He informed the counselor that he spent about 10 minutes of "think time" the first night, but decided not to do it after that. Bruce's teacher reported that he seemed like his old self and appeared much more relaxed. No additional problems or concerns were reported throughout the remainder of the school year.

Discussion. This case illustrates the benefits of altering any aspect of the performance or "doing" of a problem in order to resolve it. "Prescribing the symptom" under different conditions, such as at different times or locations, is a well-known paradoxical intervention for anxiety and other mood problems (Ascher, 1989; Frankl, 1975). Often times, the very act of trying not to think about something leads to more thinking about it (Hayes & Melancon, 1989).

Bruce was stuck in a repetitive problem pattern in which the harder he tried not to think about the breakup, the more he thought about it. The intervention successfully blocked this pattern while honoring and acknowledging the importance of the breakup for Bruce. In this sense, the intervention matched his "concerned and worried" position more closely than other people's suggestion to "get over it."

When Less is More

A seventh grader named Angela was described as a "constant nuisance" to the principal, teachers, counselors, and anyone else who would listen to her lengthy complaints about how other students bothered her. On a typical school day, she talked to three or four staff members for several minutes at a time about these concerns. After investigating the situation and finding no major support for her accusations about other students, the school counselor and various teachers talked with her numerous times to offer support and understanding in an attempt to discover the "real problem" underlying such behavior. Her complaints increased despite these efforts. Other than these complaints, she reportedly demonstrated adequate school performance. Angela's seventh-grade school counselor (Ms. Rodriguez) requested consultation from another counselor.

Ms. Rodriguez and Angela's teachers were identified as the customers for change, and their goal was to reduce the frequency of Angela's complaints. They agreed to present a message to Angela in the form of a short letter, summarized as follows:

Dear Angela,
We've discussed how frustrated we are that we cannot give you and your complaints our closest attention when you talk to us about them during class time and in the hallways. We have an idea that will give you the respect and attention you deserve. Ms. Rodriguez has agreed to reserve five minutes a day just for you to talk with her about anything you wish. You can report to her office immediately following fifth period on any day you choose to. We're very pleased that we could arrange this for you.

Every teacher reported an immediate and marked decrease in complaining, and several said that they did not hear another complaint the rest of the year. Angela met with the counselor 3 days the first week, and approximately once a week after that. Although some meetings included the familiar complaints, they were infrequent and less dramatic than previous complaints.

Discussion. This case highlights several key features of solution-focused counseling. The principle of parsimony, or "keeping it simple," is based on the idea that a small change in any aspect of the problem pattern often leads to larger changes. In this regard, the letter intervention was simple, time-effective, and cost-effective. These features are particularly relevant to busy school professionals. The specific goal of intervention was to reduce the frequency of Angela's complaints. Therefore, no attempt was made to collect detailed information regarding her past, family background, personality type, and so forth. Instead of repeating the theme of previous solution attempts by trying to uncover the real underlying problem of her complaints, the problem pattern was altered by scheduling daily 5-minute counseling sessions and limiting the number of school staff involved. Perhaps most important, the intervention appeared to fit the "nurturing" position of school personnel, and the "urgent and serious" position expressed by Angela.

To Skip or Not to Skip, That Is the Question

William was an academically talented student in jeopardy of not graduating as a result of high absenteeism from school. In an effort to persuade him to attend school and complete more school work, his teachers and parents urged him to be more responsible and take things more seriously. In addition to these verbal persuasion strategies, various incentive methods had been attempted to no avail. For example, his parents promised to pay for part of a summer vacation when he graduated if he attended school on a regular basis throughout the remainder of the year. William's school attendance had become a daily topic with his parents and several of his teachers. He was referred for counseling in late March of his senior year.

Everybody who was involved in the situation, including William, expressed their frustration and desire to change it. The counselor suggested that the parents and teachers temporarily refrain from discussing school attendance with William in order to "let the dust settle" and allow the counselor to gather more information. This temporary "refrain from action" strategy served to interrupt their existing solution attempts with a rationale that was acceptable to them.

During the first meeting, William expressed a dilemma when asked what he wanted from counseling. He wanted to graduate, yet he greatly enjoyed skipping school with his friends. The benefits of skipping were candidly discussed. Questions such as, "What are the disadvantages of attending school?" were intended to acknowledge his ambivalence regarding school attendance, and to talk with him about this issue in a way that was distinctly different than what he was used to. Exploring the "disadvantages of change" is a classic MRI strategy (Fisch et al., 1982) for reducing resistance by acknowledging the difficulty and ambivalence that clients often associate with change.

Exceptions to the problem were explored by questions such as, "How do you manage to get yourself to school on certain days despite the strong urge to skip?" These questions also introduced a different element by shifting the focus of conversation from what he was not doing to what he *was* doing to accomplish his goal of graduating. These strategies were not viewed as superior to previous parent and teacher methods in any absolute sense, but were used because they differed markedly from the previous solution attempts of verbal persuasion and lecturing.

William's school attendance improved from 40 percent (January through March) to 80 percent (April and May) following the initial counseling session. When asked what he attributed the change to, William said that he finally realized he was just "screwing himself" and that he would not graduate unless he "got his act together" and started to attend school more often. Interestingly, these were the very points or lessons that his parents and teachers tried to convey to him. Perhaps the counselor's cooperative versus coercive approach allowed William to shift from defending his position and autonomy to more clearly examining his choices and goals regarding school attendance and graduation. William was also asked about how he resisted the urge to skip, to which he replied, "I remind myself how awful it would be to work at a fast food restaurant the rest of my life, and that helps me make it to school." William graduated with the rest of his class in June.

Discussion. It is unclear exactly which aspect of intervention contributed more significantly to success in this case. From the standpoint of interrupting the problem pattern by "doing something different," the parents and teachers discontinued their usual lectures. In addition, the counselor's approach to the problem was very different than that of previous solution attempts. Instead of lecturing or arguing with William regarding the irrationality of his choice to skip school, the counselor cooperated with his perspective and asked him *why he attended school at all*, given how much fun he had skipping. Cooperating with a student's perspective is very different than agreeing with it or encouraging it. Cooperation is simply more effective than coercion in dealing with most middle and high school problems.

SUMMARY AND CONCLUSIONS

1. This is the first of two chapters on encouraging students, parents, and teachers to try something different when their existing solution attempts are not working.

2. The chapter reviewed some common attempts to resolve middle and high school problems that typically fail, and presented some unique ways to interrupt school problem patterns by doing something different.

3. The strategy of changing the doing was illustrated in case examples involving a high school student who was acting out in school and had recently broken up with his girlfriend ("The Lovesick Senior"), a middle school student who frequently complained about being harassed by other students ("When Less is More"), and a high school senior who skipped school ("To Skip or Not to Skip, That Is the Question").

The next chapter extends the theme of trying something different by describing strategies for "changing the viewing" of school problems in order to bring about solutions.

PRACTICE EXERCISES

1. Think of a problem you are currently dealing with in your own life. How have you attempted to resolve this problem? What have you or others done about the problem, and how successful have these efforts been? Do any of these attempted solutions seem to contribute to the problem instead of improving things? If so, try "doing something different." You may wish to refer to the 15 suggestions on pages 123–124 for ideas.

2. Have your partner describe a school problem in the role of a parent or teacher, and suggest a change in the performance of the problem. Switch roles to allow your partner to practice "changing the doing" in the role of the counselor.

3. Think of a school problem you are presently dealing with. Describe the problem in specific terms (who is saying/doing what to whom?; what happens next?; and so forth). How could the problem be performed differently (at a different time, in a different place, or in a different way)? How could you suggest this to your clients in a way that will be acceptable to them?

Changing the Viewing of the Problem

In general, solutions simply involve someone's doing something different or seeing something differently which leads to an increase in satisfaction.

—Steve de Shazer, *Clues*

hanging the viewing, also referred to as *reframing*, interrupts the problem pattern by introducing new and different interpretations of the problem. Because perception and behavior are interrelated, different views usually lead to different actions. Reframing strategies are based on two related assumptions:

1. There are several plausible interpretations for any given situation or behavior.
2. The current interpretations and meanings assigned to the school problem may not be as useful as others in resolving it.

Solution-focused counseling takes a very pragmatic approach to the issue of interpretation: *If one interpretation is not helping to change the problem, toss it and try a different one.*

SELECTING A DIFFERENT VIEW OF THE PROBLEM

Genius means little more than the faculty of perceiving in an unhabitual way.

—William James

To be successful, a different interpretation or view of the problem fits the facts of the situation equally well or better than the existing view, and makes sense to the student, parent, or teacher. Most school problems can be viewed in a variety of ways. Depression can be relabeled as "realistic pessimism," classroom misbehavior as "a unique way of communicating," and adolescent rebellion as "necessary steps toward personal responsibility." In many cases, reframing attaches a positive connotation to a behavior or person that is usually viewed in a negative way. Box 9.1 provides some examples of this.

Although reframing in schools often focuses on the behavior of students, it can also be used to offer students a different view of their parents or teachers. For example, in situations of parent–adolescent conflict, the student might be encouraged to view the parents' behavior as "caring and committed" instead of "controlling and insensitive." Likewise, desired changes in a student's classroom behavior may occur when a student changes his or her view of the teacher from "mean and bossy" to "concerned and structured."

There is a variety of options for changing the way a school problem is viewed. These options can be drawn from two main sources: (1) content provided by theories of counseling and psychology, and (2) unique content provided by clients. Frequently, content from both of these sources is combined into a new meaning or "frame" for the problem.

Content Provided By Theories

Solution-focused counseling is not wedded to any one particular theory of counseling or psychology. Therefore, the content from *any* theoretical perspective is fair game, as long as it fits the facts of the situation and makes sense to the client. For example, the theory of self psychology (Kohut, 1980) suggests that adolescents' unusual or annoying behavior often represents their attempt to meet a normal developmental need for affirmation and recognition. If accepted by a parent or teacher who has previously viewed such behavior as spiteful and manipulative, this new interpretation might lead to more effective ways to respond to the behavior.

Content Provided by Clients

Like every other aspect of solution-focused counseling, reframing seeks to include as much of the client as possible. The case of Maria provides an exam-

---

Box 9.1. Reframing Problems By Offering Positive Connotations

Controlling = Providing structure and direction

Defiant = Independent, assertive, committed

Argumentative = Caring enough to disagree

Immature = Fun-hearted, playful

Impulsive = Spontaneous, energetic

Withdrawn = Introspective, contemplative, observant

Passive = Ability to accept things as they are, laid back

Rigid = Steadfast and committed to a plan of action

---

ple of how the ideas and comments of clients can be incorporated into an alternative view of the problem. Maria was referred for counseling by her teachers because of classroom behavior problems. She was frequently assigned to after-school detention, and was suspended from school on two separate occasions. When asked about any possible disadvantages of improving her behavior, she said that her classmates might be disappointed if she did not clown around and make them laugh in class. We discussed this for a few minutes, at which point I offered a different interpretation based on Maria's comments. I asked Maria how much longer she would be willing to sacrifice her own freedom in order to entertain her classmates, adding that it was unusually generous of a high school student to do this. She seemed intrigued by this interpretation, and commented that she had never thought of her misbehavior as being "generous." As we discussed this further, she became more and more determined not to "sacrifice her own freedom" for the sake of other students. The session ended with a discussion of other ways that Maria could keep her friends without getting into trouble. As illustrated in this example, alternative interpretations of a school problem have a good chance of being accepted when they originate from unique content provided by the client.

PRESENTING A DIFFERENT VIEW OF THE PROBLEM

In most cases, a different view of the school problem should be presented in a tentative manner in order to convey the client's freedom to accept or reject the new view, and to allow the counselor maximum flexibility in presenting other views should the client reject it. The following phrases can be used to present alternative views of the problem in a respectful, tentative manner:

- I'm not sure this is on target. See what you think.
- You're the best judge of what might help explain this, so I want to run something by you to see what you think.
- Tell me whether or not you think this is in the ballpark.
- I'm curious what you think of this idea.
- Do you think it's possible that . . .
- Some people would say that . . . (this is particularly useful in presenting theory-based views)

It is important to assess the client's reaction as we are presenting an alternative view. People may indicate their interest by leaning forward in the chair, raising their eyebrows, and nodding their head "yes." In addition to observing these nonverbal responses, the following questions are useful in assessing the client's reaction to reframing:

- Does that makes any sense to you?
- What do you think of that?
- Do you think there might be something to that?
- Is that a possibility?

CASE EXAMPLES OF CHANGING THE VIEWING

Any story one may tell about anything is better understood by considering other possible ways in which it could be told.

—J. Bruner, 1987

The following examples illustrate how reframing can be successfully applied to a variety of middle and high school problems.

Desperate and Developmental

She sobbed as she described her depression and shame. This was my third meeting with Jane, a 16-year-old student referred to counseling primarily for academic difficulties in two of her classes, English and history. The previous two meetings had dealt primarily with these difficulties, along with some conflicts she and her mother were having at home.

Jane said that she had to tell somebody about her problem. She had not slept well for the past 2 weeks since the problem began. She was falling further behind in her school work and having more trouble concentrating in her classes. She prefaced her description of the problem by saying that she viewed herself as a disgusting person, and that I would undoubtedly view her this way after she told me what she had done. With great difficulty, Jane told me that she had "talked nasty" on the telephone to a male friend on three separate occasions during the past couple of weeks. She was convinced that she was a "sexual deviant" or had a "multiple personality."

Previous meetings revealed that it was not unusual for Jane to be grounded and restricted to her house for 1 or 2 weeks at a time for things like coming home late or "talking back" to her mother. While grounded, Jane was required to be in the house at all times except during school, including weekends. She was also prohibited from talking with friends on the phone. Jane lived at home with her mother, who had refused two earlier invitations to meet with me to discuss Jane's school performance and conflicts at home.

Aside from the questionable parental practice of marathon groundings, over which Jane and I had very little control, it was obvious that Jane's view of the problem was not helping her in school or in any other part of her life. After a few minutes of silence during which she continued to sob and stare at the floor, I offered an alternative interpretation of her phone calls. I suggested to Jane that her behavior, although understandably scary and confusing to her, might actually represent a *natural* attempt to meet a *normal* and *typical* adolescent need for "lively interaction" with peers, and to deal with the *common* sexual curiosity that accompanies adolescence. Unlike most of her peers, Jane's access to normal teenage activities and interactions was severely restricted. I explained that these extreme restrictions might have prompted her to resort to extreme measures. In this sense, the phone calls represented Jane's desperate yet understandable attempts to "experience adolescence" in the face of groundings and other restrictions that prevented her from doing so in more conventional ways.

When I asked Jane what she thought of this explanation, she said that it made some sense to her. She was visibly relieved to learn that she was not crazy after all. Within a few minutes, we began discussing how she could improve her grades in English and history. No further mention was made of the telephone problem during two subsequent meetings throughout the remainder of the school year.

Discussion. "Changing the viewing" requires the counselor's flexibility in developing and selecting alternative views that fit the facts of the situation and are plausible to the client. There is nothing inherently magical or right about the developmental interpretation that was used to reframe the problem in this case. If Jane had rejected it, it would have been discarded, regardless of how insightful or plausible it appeared to me. The "developmental frame" was effective in this case because it fit the facts, Jane accepted it, and it introduced something different into the problem pattern.

Giving Them What They Want

Zach, a 17-year-old senior, was referred in February by the school principal and his teachers for "oppositional behavior and defiance of authority." He frequently refused to do school work, and liberally shared his negative opinions regarding the school, the teachers, and the principal (Mr. Billingsly). After reviewing school records and interviewing the principal and teachers, the counselor met with Zach.

Counselor: I've already talked to your teachers and Mr. Billingsly about what they see happening...

Zach: Huh! I bet that was great. Did they tell you what an asshole I am?

Counselor: Not exactly.

Zach: I'm surprised. They need to straighten this school out. That's the problem. This school sucks, along with most of the people in it. Now I have to come and talk to you like it's my fault.

[*Zach resented being referred for counseling, and viewed it as yet another attempt to "blame him" for everything that goes wrong in the classroom or at the school. As illustrated next, the counselor accepts and works within this view instead of challenging it.*]

Counselor: What sucks the most for you about the school?

Zach: Almost everything. There are *some* cool teachers, and I've got some friends, but most of the teachers can't teach. You just sit there. Then they go ballistic when you mess around or don't do your work. Now I have to come here like it's my fault.

Counselor: Do you do your work?

Zach: Some of it.

Counselor: Do you do more of it in certain classes?

Zach: It depends. I really don't care about it. I just want to get the hell out of this school.

Counselor: How are you going to do that?

Zach: Just graduate.

Counselor: I mean, as far as credits go, do you have to pass most of your classes to have enough credits to graduate?

Zach: I have to pass every one of my classes this year.

Counselor: Are you going to be able to do that?

Zach: The classes are pretty easy. Well, most of them are. But the last time I got suspended, I missed an English test and she wouldn't let me retake it. So now I'm failing English.

Counselor: Are you failing anything else?

Zach: I might be failing history. I don't know.

Counselor: What happens if you don't pass these classes? Do you have to wait to graduate or take them in the summer?

Zach: I'm not taking them in the summer. No way.

Counselor: If you failed a class or two, would you just forget it and drop out?

Zach: Probably. For a while, anyway. I really don't want to do that. I mean, I made it this far. I don't know how [*laughs*].

Counselor: How do you think you made it this far, with all the detentions and suspensions?

Zach: I'm pretty smart. They don't think so. I just don't suck up to the teachers like some kids. I don't raise my hand a lot in class.

Counselor: Who doesn't think you're smart?

Zach: Most of the teachers. And Mr. Billingsly [the principal]. Especially Billingsly. He thinks I'm a waste. He just waits for me to screw up so he can call my parents and give me detention. I don't care. I'm going to do what I want. He doesn't scare me.

After a few more minutes of discussion, it was evident that Zach wanted to graduate, if only to "get the hell out of the school." It was also clear that he perceived the principal and a couple of teachers as "out to get him." Zach held the following position: "I'm going to do what I want no matter what Mr. Billingsly and the teachers say or do to me." He held to this position very strongly, and any attempt to encourage him to view things differently would have to take this position into account.

The situation resembled the MRI problem process in that each party continued to respond with "more of the same" despite ineffective results. The problem pattern typically was initiated when Zach was reprimanded for some disciplinary infraction in the classroom, often receiving an in-class punishment in the form of extra assignments. Zach frequently questioned the fairness of the punishment and refused to do it, resulting in a trip to the principal's office. Mr. Billingsly, the principal, usually tried to reason with Zach by explaining that he could make it much easier on himself if he would just take the teacher's punishment without making such a scene. Zach would then tell Mr. Billingsly to "shove it" or something similar, and that he was going to do what *he* wanted. The meetings usually resulted in Mr. Billingsly calling Zach's parents and assigning additional days of detention. Zach's parents told Mr. Billingsly that they had talked with their son on numerous occasions about his school problems, and withheld car privileges several times in an attempt to improve his school behavior to no avail. The parents were at their wit's end and out of ideas.

The more Zach misbehaved, the more he was punished. The more he was punished, the more convinced he became that the principal and teachers were out to get him. This led to even more misbehavior based on Zach's view that "they aren't going to break me." In the following excerpt, the counselor offers an alternative view of the situation in an effort to interrupt the problem cycle and promote a different response to the problem. The facts of the situation are reframed in a way that is intended to promote different behavior by utilizing Zach's strong determination to not give in and let them win.

Counselor: You mentioned that Mr. Billingsly and some of your teachers are out to get you.

Zach: Right.

Counselor: They don't like you, right?

Zach: That's putting it mild.

Counselor: Okay. It seems like you might be giving them what they want. You're playing right into their hands.

Zach: What do you mean?

Counselor: You're doing exactly what they want you to do by giving them an excuse to get rid of you and suspend you for good. You're close to the edge right now of getting suspended, right?

Zach: Yeah.

Counselor: If things keep going like this, and you keep getting sucked into this trap of mouthing off and getting sent to the office, then you'll get suspended soon and they win. You're gone. They win. [*Zach seemed genuinely curious about this and the counselor continued.*] It's like a card game. As long as you keep doing what you're doing, getting sent out of class and getting detention, you're playing right into their hands. They're holding all the cards right now.

Zach: I don't know about that.

Counselor: I don't either, but it's something to think about. You want to graduate, and you won't if you keep giving them a legitimate reason to nail you. Something to think about.

Zach received only two detentions the next week compared to an average of four per week during the previous month. The next conversation occurred at the end of the week in which Zach received two detentions.

Counselor: So, what's different about this week?
Zach: Nothing, really.
Counselor: Did you think any more about what we talked about?
Zach: Yeah. I guess I kind of see what you mean. But they're not going to stop me from graduating.
Counselor: How are you going to make sure they don't stop you from graduating?

Zach continued receiving occasional detentions, but not nearly as many as he had during the month preceding intervention. He received a 3-day suspension 1 month following this meeting, but remained in school and passed all his classes (including English and history, both of which he barely passed with a grade of D). Zach graduated on time with the rest of his class.

Discussion. The alternative view interrupted the problem cycle by altering the way Zach perceived the situation. Another noteworthy aspect of this case was the fact that my own personal perceptions of the situation were very different than Zach's. I viewed Mr. Billingsly, the principal, as very caring and reasonable in his dealings with Zach. However, the counselor's or anyone else's opinion is always secondary to the client's opinion in solution-focused counseling. Counselors can effectively accept and accommodate a client's opinion without necessarily agreeing with it. The counseling process was adapted to Zach's views and "culture" instead of trying to convince him that Mr. Billingsly was not such a bad guy after all. Any such attempt would have probably brought the counseling process to a screeching halt, because Zach would have viewed counseling as simply another attempt to make him look like the bad guy.

A Wake-Up Call From the Unconscious

An 11th-grade student named Jessica was referred because of "concentration problems" and a sudden decline in academic performance. When asked if anything in her life had changed to coincide with the onset of these difficulties, she said that she had been very distressed about recurring nightmares in which she was being chased by someone. She tried to avoid falling asleep so she would not have the dream. Of course, this kept her up later at night and made it harder to concentrate in school. This strategy did not reduce the nightmares, according to Jessica. She stated that she had similar dreams a few years earlier, but that she was not nearly as concerned and scared about them then as she was now. She felt like she was "going crazy." Jessica's view of herself and the situation appeared to be contributing to the problem instead of helping to resolve it.

When asked what she wanted from counseling, Jessica said she wanted to stop having the dreams so she could "start having a normal life again." She was interested in dreams, and believed that dreams could be very instructive in people's lives. Jessica expressed a strong desire to understand the meaning of her dreams and of her intense fear regarding them. When the counselor asked about her current interpretation, Jessica explained that she viewed her dreams and related fears as signs of weakness, regression, and immaturity. She said that she had grown up a lot in the last couple years, and that these dreams were a kickback to a younger age when she was less mature and used to have the same kind of dreams. Jessica viewed her fears as unjustified and irrational because she knew that she could not really be hurt by someone in a dream. Although these interpretations were not very satisfactory or helpful to her, they were the only views that she could think of to explain her dreams and related fears.

Based on the information provided by Jessica, the counselor invited her to consider a different interpretation. During the past year, she had become very busy at school and with her friends. The counselor suggested that she had become so busy that she may have taken her growth for granted and not properly acknowledged it. The dreams, therefore, might be serving as a wake-up call or reminder from the unconscious to "stop and smell the roses," that is, to take the time to acknowledge and give herself credit for the gains and progress she had recently made in her life. Jessica looked intrigued, and the counselor continued. Her fears regarding these dreams were explained by the notion that she presently had much more to lose than she did when she had similar dreams a few years ago. The thought of being chased and killed by someone is justifiably more frightening when you have more to live for. Therefore, as unpleasant as the dreams and fears were, they could be viewed as signs of how much better Jessica's life was now as compared to a few years back.

Not only did Jessica accept this new interpretation or "frame," she extended it by adding that she took much better care of herself now than she used to in terms of hygiene and diet. She also said that she rarely gave herself credit for anything good that happened in her life. Jessica did not report any further concerns regarding the dreams, and her grades and concentration improved to their previous level.

Discussion. Effective reframing offers a different view of the problem that fits the client and the facts of the situation. In this case, the new view incorporated content provided by Jessica into an interpretation that was very different from her existing explanation of her dreams and fears. Viewing the dreams as unconscious reminders (versus signs of craziness), and fears as indications of recent growth and maturity (versus weakness and regression), introduced a difference that made a difference.

Pervert or Parent Protector?

A sixth grader named Steve was referred for counseling after making some "obscene remarks and gestures" toward one of his teachers (Ms. Taylor). The counselor met with Steve and his grandparents during the second day of a 1-week suspension from school. Counseling was requested by school personnel in order to obtain a professional opinion of Steve's mental stability and "sexual problem." School officials also wanted a determination regarding the likelihood that Steve would repeat such incidents in the future.

Steve was living with his grandparents at the time of the meeting, and had been moving back and forth between his father and grandparents for the past year. His grandparents explained that he was a "nice, polite boy." They proudly added that he occasionally helped out with household chores without even being asked.

Grandfather: He's never used foul language with us or done anything like this. I don't know why he did it.

Counselor: Steve, do you have any theories about why you did it?

Steve: [*shrugs shoulders*] No.

Counselor: How well do you get along with Ms. Taylor?

Steve: Not real good.

Counselor: On a scale of 1 to 10, 1 being "really bad" and 10 being "great," where would you rate it?

Steve: About a 2 or a 1.

Counselor: Where would you put your other teachers?

Steve: 5 or 6.

Counselor: So you definitely clash more with Ms. Taylor than the other teachers.

Steve: Yeah.

Counselor: How important is it to you, again on a scale of 1 to 10, to get along with your teachers at school?

Steve: About 5.

Counselor: How important do you think it is for Ms. Taylor to get along with you?

Steve: Probably a 1. She doesn't like me. She never liked me in the first place. She's got two or three teacher's pets in that room. She always lets them do everything.

After a few minutes of discussion regarding specific aspects of his relationship with Ms. Taylor, the following "frame" was offered to Steve and his grandparents.

Counselor: You mentioned getting along a lot better with your other teachers than Ms. Taylor. I don't know if this is on target or not, but perhaps it was no accident that you said and did these things in Ms. Taylor's room instead of some other room. Maybe this was your way of trying to draw her attention away from her favorite students, the teacher's pets, and onto you and some other students. Granted, it's not your everyday way of asking for attention, but still, I'm just wondering. What do you think of that?

Steve: I don't care what she thinks of me. She doesn't like me. I don't like her either. It doesn't bother me.

Counselor: [*turning to Steve's grandparents*] What do you think?

Grandmother: I don't know. Like you said, that's a pretty weird way to get attention. I think he's smarter than that.

This alternative view was clearly not acceptable to Steve, and his grandmother's response was lukewarm at best. These responses prompted the counselor to drop this interpretation and move on to something else. The following dialogue occurred later in the meeting while discussing how often Steve saw his father (Don), and how they spent their time together.

Counselor: So, you guys watch TV a lot together.

Steve: Yeah.

Grandfather: You know, I keep telling Donnie to take him places and do things with him, like to the park or ball games, but I can't get through to him. Donnie has had a lot of problems himself. He hasn't held a steady job for a couple years, and he drinks a lot.

While the grandfather continued to describe the difficulties and shortcomings of Steve's father, Steve looked downward and appeared as if he was about to cry.

Counselor: Steve, you really care about your Dad, don't you?

Steve: [*nods head "yes," still looking downward*]

Counselor: Do you help him a lot like you help your grandparents?

Steve: [*nods head "yes"*]

Counselor: That's impressive. A lot of kids your age don't even think about helping their parents. It wouldn't even cross their mind to think of helping out at home.

Grandfather: Another thing is, Donnie gets these magazines like *Playboy*, and leaves them sitting around the house. I keep telling him that Steve doesn't need to be seeing that stuff, but he keeps doing it. That's probably where Steve gets these ideas.

Counselor: What do you think, Steve?

Steve: That stuff doesn't bother me. I can see that stuff anywhere. It's not like I'm a pervert or something.

Counselor: That stuff is available a lot these days. Besides, books or no books, clean house or messy house, you still care a whole lot about your Dad, don't you? [*Steve nods "yes"; counselor turns to grandparents*] Some people would say that Steve is actually trying to protect his father by getting in trouble and drawing attention *to* himself and *away from* Donnie. [*Steve looks somewhat in-*

terested; the counselor continues to address the grandparents] If you, your wife, and the school people keep focusing on Steve's problems, then maybe you won't criticize Donnie as much, and Donnie might feel better about himself. Steve might have done this school problem to get everybody to "back off" and stop criticizing his father. Also, this is one way for Steve to get his Dad to pay more attention to him. For example, when this happened, the school called Donnie and he had to come up to school to get Steve. Steve, what did you do that day after your Dad picked you up from school?

Steve: We went back to his house.

Counselor: What did he say about what happened at school?

Steve: He yelled at me some. He told me I better not do it anymore.

Counselor: Do you think he meant it?

Steve: I know he meant it. He was really mad.

Counselor: He was really acting like a dad, wasn't he?

Steve: Yeah. He was acting like my grandpa. [*grandparents laugh*]

Counselor: What are some other ways you could get his attention and get him to act more like a dad?

Steve: I don't know.

Counselor: I'm just wondering, because it seems like there might be some other ways to do that besides getting yourself suspended from school.

The conversation continued to explore different ways that Steve might support his father and get his father's attention besides misbehaving in school. The grandparents agreed not to criticize Don in Steve's presence, and to encourage Don to spend more quality time with Steve. Steve returned to school the next week, and no further incidents were reported during the remaining two months of the school year.

Discussion. This case highlights several important features of reframing. First, the decision to abandon or stay with a reframing intervention is based strictly on the client's response. Neither Steve nor his grandparents thought much of the idea that Steve's misbehavior might have been an attempt to secure the teacher's attention. Therefore, it was immediately dropped, and the counselor offered a different interpretation later in the session. The notion that a child's behavior problem might serve specific functions within the family is based on the structural theory of family therapy (Minuchin, 1974). This theory, combined with information provided by Steve and his grandparents, provided the content for a reframing intervention that fit the facts, yet differed markedly from the prevailing notion that there was something wrong or perverse in Steve himself.

SUMMARY AND CONCLUSIONS

1. Changing the viewing, or reframing, encourages students, teachers, and parents to adopt alternative views of a school problem. Because percep-

tion and behavior are interrelated, changes in the meaning or interpretation of a problem typically lead to behavioral changes as well.

2. In order to be effective, alternative views or meanings of the problem must fit the facts as well or better than existing views, and make sense to the clients. Theories of psychology and counseling, as well as material supplied by clients themselves, provide useful content for changing the viewing of school problems. Reframing often invites people to consider a more positive connotation of their own behavior, or the behavior of others.

3. Changing the viewing of middle and high school problems was illustrated by case examples of a girl who was depressed and ashamed ("Desperate and Developmental"), an "oppositional and defiant" high school senior ("Giving Them What They Want"), a student who complained of nightmares ("A Wake-Up Call From the Unconscious"), and a middle school student who was suspended for making "nasty gestures" to a teacher ("Pervert or Parent Protector?").

This was the last of four chapters describing specific solution-focused interventions for school problems. The next chapter presents some suggestions for when and how to end counseling.

PRACTICE EXERCISES

1. Have your partner present a school problem, and practice "changing the viewing" by offering an alternative interpretation or explanation of the problem. Switch roles to allow your partner to practice the strategy of reframing.

2. Review a list of common descriptors of school problems (disruptive, impulsive, and so forth), and provide a positive connotation for each descriptor. Most behavior rating scales include an ample number of negative descriptors that could be used for this purpose.

3. Think of an actual problem you are currently experiencing. How do you and other people typically respond to the problem? What actions are being taken in response to the problem, and how effective are they? How do you or others currently view the situation? Think of some different, plausible views of the situation. Of these alternative views, which one(s) might lead to different actions in response to the problem?

When and How to End Counseling

The aim of realistic, responsible therapy can only be an increased skill in dealing with life problems as they arise, but not a problem-free life.

—P. Watzlawick, *The Language of Change*

This chapter offers some guidelines and strategies to consider in deciding when and how to end counseling. These considerations are offered in the hope that practitioners will adapt them to suit their own style and circumstances.

GUIDELINES AND STRATEGIES FOR TERMINATING COUNSELING

Some circumstances may prevent counselors from having the luxury or opportunity to consider issues regarding when and how to end counseling. Counseling sometimes ends when a student moves to a different school. Administrative and other noncounseling job duties make it difficult to do a lot of counseling in the first place, much less to assess carefully when to end counseling with a particular student, teacher, or parent. In other words, termination decisions are sometimes made for us. This is simply one of the realities of school counseling over which practitioners have little control.

Viewing Every Session As the Last

Time constraints and other practical realities of school counseling support the recommendation to approach every counseling session as if it were the last. As emphasized throughout this book, *every* contact with a student, parent, or teacher offers possibilities for change. Solutions can emerge at any point in the counseling process. Approaching each session as if it were the last helps counselors and clients remain focused on specific goals and alert to small signs of success.

Using Goals As Guidelines

Goals are the most useful guidelines for deciding when to end counseling. Termination decisions are aided by beginning with the end in mind and developing small, specific goals at the outset of counseling. In addition to enabling counselors and clients to detect small improvements throughout counseling, small goals make the task of terminating counseling easier and more effective.

The function of solution-focused counseling in schools is to help people resolve specific school problems, not necessarily to make their lives problem-free in every respect. Helping people change a specific school problem is hard enough, and it is unrealistic for school practitioners to take on much more than that. Being very clear with ourselves and our clients about the goals and scope of school counseling helps in making effective termination decisions.

Terminating When Clients Are "On Track"

A complete resolution of the problem is not required for termination. Instead, termination should be considered when clients are on track toward resolving the problem and have a clear understanding of what they are doing successfully. These decisions are aided by clear goal criteria established at the start of counseling. Questions such as, "How will we know when counseling is no longer needed?" and "What will this student be doing when things start getting better?," are useful in establishing specific goal criteria and in deciding when to end counseling.

Collaborating and Leaving the Door Open

Like every other phase of solution-focused counseling, termination should be a collaborative decision between the practitioner and client(s). The following excerpt illustrates a collaborative way to approach the topic of termination, while leaving the door open for future contacts.

Counselor: I'm really impressed with the changes you've made, and it seems to me that you have a good sense of what you need to do to continue such changes. How do you feel about that?

Student: I know I've got to keep doing homework to pass, and not mouth off in class like I used to.

Counselor: With these changes you've made, along with your plans to keep doing what's working for you, what would you think about us not meeting each week like we have been?

Student: That's okay, but if I start messing up, can we meet again?

Counselor: Sure. In fact, we can plan to meet again in a month or so to visit for a few minutes and check up on things. How does that sound?

Student: Fine.

Counselor: If you want to meet before then, just let me know.

Terminating With Students Who Do Not Want To

Some students want to continue meeting even after they have made sufficient improvements and are on track toward continued success. The following steps are useful in these situations. First, counselors can express appreciation for the student's willingness and desire to continue. The counselor can also add that it takes a great deal of courage and stamina to discuss one's problems with others and to take steps toward resolving them. Second, practitioners can explain that they are required to help several other students who are experiencing major difficulties in school much like those that the client experienced. This is intended to promote empathy between the student who wants to continue and the students who are awaiting counseling services. Third, the counselor can ask students and parents if they would be willing for the counselor to call upon them in the future for their ideas and suggestions on helping others deal with situations similar to those that they have successfully changed. With students, this request is sometimes made by offering them membership in the Consultant Club, which is composed of former students who have demonstrated expertise in overcoming school problems. Finally, offering students and others an open door for future contacts seems to reduce their apprehension regarding the termination of counseling.

Termination is the last in a series of interrelated steps comprising the solution-focused counseling process. Appendix E summarizes these steps in order to help "put it all together."

SUMMARY AND CONCLUSIONS

The decision to terminate counseling can be a difficult one. I hope that the guidelines in this chapter will help you and your clients make effective decisions about when and how to end counseling.

PRACTICE EXERCISES

1. Think of a case in which counseling was successfully terminated, and consider what you did to contribute to this success.
2. With a partner serving as the client and you as the counselor, conduct a short counseling session as if it will be your first and last session. Note any differences in your approach to this session and your usual approach.
3. What are some methods that you have used, or thought of using, to deal with situations in which students do not want to terminate counseling?

Troubleshooting and
Getting Started

11

When Things Don't Go As Planned: 10 Troubleshooting Tips

Failure is the opportunity to begin again more intelligently.

—Henry Ford

M ost books, this one included, present successful cases in order to demonstrate the rationale and intended effect of various strategies. Although the cases in this book are real, things do not always work out this way in everyday practice. Counseling occasionally stalls. People do not always accept and implement the counselor's suggestions. Strategies that are supposed to work according to a theory or textbook do not always work.

This chapter offers a troubleshooting guide in the form of 10 questions. Many of these questions, along with related strategies for getting counseling back on track, are adapted from Walter and Peller (1992) and O'Hanlon and Weiner-Davis (1989).

1. How Interested Is the Client in Changing the Problem?

This is an important initial question to consider when counseling is not progressing, especially in working with adolescents. Because students are typically referred for counseling by someone else, they may not be very interested in changing the problem. In fact, they may not even acknowledge that a problem exists. One of the most frequent stumbling blocks in counseling adolescents is trying to convince them that they have a problem when they do not think they do. Treating visitors like customers is a common impediment to the success of counseling with middle and high school students, parents, and teachers.

2. Is There a Stated Goal of Counseling?

Goal-related considerations are crucial to successful troubleshooting. The most fundamental issue regarding a counseling goal is whether or not you have one in the first place. Several years ago, I complained to a colleague about one of my high school counseling cases that was going nowhere. After patiently listening for a few minutes, my colleague asked: "What is the stated goal?" I immediately realized that there was no stated goal in this case. No wonder it felt like we were going around in circles! The essence of this troubleshooting guideline is captured in the saying, "If you don't know where you're going, you'll probably end up somewhere else."

3. Is the Goal Specific, Clear, and Reasonable?

Vague and unrealistic goals can impede counseling progress, as can the counselor's or client's expectation that large changes will occur instantly. Although solution-focused counseling is designed to promote change as efficiently as possible, some changes occur at a slow pace and in small increments. Counselors and clients may overlook small improvements in a chronic problem situation because they are so used to "seeing the problem." Specific, reasonable goals help clients and counselors recognize and build on small changes.

4. Whose Goal Is It?

Once you have determined that the counseling goal is clear and reasonable, consider whose goal it is. The further counselors stray from the words and ideas that clients use in describing what they want from counseling, the less meaningful the goal is likely to be for them. Middle and high school students who are unwilling to take action on someone else's goal ("to make the student more responsible") may be very willing to act on a goal that is worded to fit their position and preferences ("to gain more car privileges and freedom at home"). When counselors find themselves working harder than the client, this may be a signal that the goal is more important to them than it is to the client. It is helpful in these situations to renegotiate the goal to make it more meaningful to the client.

5. Is the Client Apprehensive or Ambivalent About Change?

Some people are apprehensive and ambivalent about change (Duncan, 1989). For example, a student may truly want to change the school problem, and yet may feel somewhat uneasy about the new and unfamiliar experiences that change will bring. For cautious and ambivalent clients, it is helpful to employ two general interventions suggested by the MRI model (Fisch et al., 1982): (1) suggest that the client go slow in making changes, and (2) inquire about the disadvantages of change. Both strategies promote change while acknowledging and validating the person's apprehension or ambivalence.

"Go slow" interventions are particularly effective with apprehensive clients who view change as overwhelming and highly improbable. The suggestion to "take it slow and not rush change" is intended to connect with and relieve people's apprehension, permitting them to pursue change at a pace that is comfortable for them. Asking students about the potential drawbacks or disadvantages of change acknowledges and validates their ambivalence. Consider Kevin, a ninth-grade student who responded to this question by stating that he goofed off in class in order to make his friends laugh, and that he would be letting them down if he stopped. His classroom behavior improved markedly after we candidly discussed this disadvantage of change, along with other ways that he could be a good friend without getting in trouble.

6. Is Counseling Respecting and Accommodating the Client's Language, Position, and Experience?

Progress is impeded when we fail to adequately consider and accommodate the client's language, position, and experience regarding the problem. Solution-focused counselors can become overzealous in their attempts to be upbeat and positive to the point of ignoring or minimizing important aspects of the problem and the pain associated with it. Failing to properly acknowledge the client's problem and his or her experience of it is a common tendency in many people's early attempts at applying solution-focused counseling. When things are stuck in solution-focused counseling, it is important to consider whether your interactions with a client are "solution-focused" or "solution-forced" (Nylund & Corsiglia, 1994).

7. Is Counseling Seen By the Client as Something Different or More Of the Same?

The success of counseling is greatly jeopardized by doing more of the same interventions that have already proven ineffective in resolving the problem. Consider a situation in which a high school student has been lectured extensively by parents and teachers regarding the negative consequences of school truancy to no avail. In these cases, it is inadvisable for counselors to point out additional consequences of truancy such as salaries of high school dropouts or other issues that may not have been adequately covered by the parents or teachers. As useful as counselors may deem this information to be, their "lecturing posture" closely resembles the theme of previous solution attempts and will likely have the same result. When counseling is going in circles instead of moving forward, ask yourself and the client if counseling is being perceived as more of the same. If it is, then try something different.

8. Is My View of the Client Helping or Hindering Progress?

The objective facts of a school problem are fairly clear-cut. However, the meanings and explanations of these facts are quite negotiable and flexible. Some interpretations are more productive than others. For instance, the fact that a student did not implement a counselor's suggestion can be seen as either "resistance" or "useful communication and feedback" to the counselor regarding the need for a different intervention. Viewing and responding to clients as capable and cooperative is more productive than viewing them as deficient and resistant.

9. How Is the Client Viewing the Problem, the Counselor, and the Counseling Process?

In addition to examining the usefulness of our views, it is helpful to consider the client's views of the problem, the counselor, and the counseling process. The following questions are useful in identifying relevant perceptions of the client: Does the client view the problem as "solvable" and within his or her control? Is the client sufficiently hopeful regarding solution possibilities? Does the client perceive the counselor as an ally and advocate? Does the client understand and accept the purpose and goal of counseling?

10. Is There Someone Else Who Might Provide a Fresh Perspective on This Case?

In addition to asking the client what needs to happen for counseling to be more successful, consultation with professional colleagues often provides a fresh and different perspective on a difficult case. As Walter and Peller (1989) observe: "Since we may sometimes be too close to the trees to see the forest, we may not recognize a nonproductive pattern between us and the client" (p. 258). A small suggestion or observation from a colleague can turn a case around and get counseling back on track. In addition to providing fresh ideas on difficult cases, school practitioners have reported other benefits of peer consultation, such as increased morale and job satisfaction (Zins, Maher, Murphy, & Wess, 1988).

SUMMARY AND CONCLUSIONS

This chapter presented several troubleshooting questions and strategies to consider when things do not go as planned in counseling. I hope that these ideas will assist you in dealing with the inevitable glitches that occur in the real world of school counseling. The next and final chapter offers some recommendations and encouragement for putting solution-focused counseling into practice where you work.

PRACTICE EXERCISES

1. Make a list of your current counseling cases that are progressing very slowly or not at all, and ask yourself the following goal-related questions for each case:

   - Is there a stated goal?
   - If so, is the goal clear and reasonable?
   - Does the goal belong to the client?
   - Is the goal worded in a way that fits the client's position?

2. Think of a current case in which you feel stuck. Who could you talk with about ideas and suggestions for getting unstuck? You may want to make an offer to similarly assist one of your colleagues. Perhaps you and some colleagues could schedule monthly brainstorming meetings to discuss ideas and strategies for dealing with difficult cases.

Putting Solution-Focused Counseling Into Practice

Small opportunities are often the beginning of great enterprises.

—Demosthenes

This book is not intended to cast solution-focused counseling as a panacea for school problems, or to suggest that strategies associated with traditional approaches be abandoned. Solution-focused techniques should be flexibly applied and tailored to the unique circumstances of the problem and people involved in counseling. This is easier said than done, and it takes some practice. This chapter offers ideas and suggestions for putting solution-focused counseling to work in your day-to-day professional life. These suggestions are based on common concerns and questions that I have heard in conducting solution-focused training workshops. Because you know yourself and your job better than anyone else, I encourage you to adapt these recommendations accordingly.

START WHERE YOU ARE AND TAKE IT SLOW

1. Think of what you have done, and are currently doing, to be "solution-focused" in your work.

2. Make a list entitled "Solution-Focused Things I Am Already Doing." This list could include thoughts, attitudes, and actions that are consistent with the principles and practices of solution-focused counseling.

3. Pick one item from the list and make a practical plan for developing this idea or action during the next week. Think small. If that means devoting 5 minutes to it during the upcoming week, then so be it. That's 5 minutes more than the week before, and that's progress.

4. Continue to do this with other items from the list at a pace and level that are comfortable for you.

5. Remind yourself that it is hard work to refine and expand your counseling skills, but that it can also be fun and rewarding. If you feel burdened by

trying to do too much too soon, slow down and take smaller steps. Give yourself a break. Take the time to recognize and celebrate your small victories in learning and implementing this approach. In other words, treat yourself the same way that you would treat clients in solution-focused counseling.

6. In addition to building on the solution-focused things that you are already doing, adapt the previous five steps in order to apply new ideas and strategies from this book. Pick a specific type of question, such as the miracle question or scaling, and try it out during your next meeting with a student, parent, or teacher. Evaluate its effectiveness, modify it accordingly, and try it again. Some of the strategies in this book will be more compatible with your style and circumstances than others. Take what you want and leave the rest.

7. If it is possible to collaborate with others who are interested in becoming more solution-focused, do so in whatever form possible including in-person meetings, phone calls, and e-mail. One of my most enjoyable and productive professional experiences has been participating in a solution-focused peer consultation group. We meet every other month for about 2 hours to discuss difficult cases and review materials pertaining to solution-focused counseling.

LEARN MORE ABOUT IT

Reading this book could go on your list of something you are already doing to improve your solution-focused counseling skills. You may wish to consult other sources from the list of references at the end of this book. Training in solution-focused counseling is much more available now than it was 10 years ago. Workshops on this approach may be available through professional organizations in your discipline, national and regional training agencies, and individuals who specialize in solution-focused counseling. You might also consider approaching your own school district or agency about sponsoring solution-focused training for you and your colleagues. The advantage of working with a group from a local school district or agency is that training can be specifically tailored to the unique population and circumstances of that particular setting.

PRACTICE THINKING "SOLUTION-FOCUSED"

Schools tend to recognize, analyze, and act on undesired behavior more than desired behavior. This tendency pervades much of society, including the media and helping professions. It is a hard habit to break. For this reason, I recommend that you apply solution-focused thinking and strategies to a variety of professional responsibilities in order to make it a more routine part of your work life. The following examples illustrate the broad applicability of solution-focused thinking in middle and high schools.

Dealing With Diversity

I have found the solution-focused way of thinking to be useful not only to individual and group counseling per se, but to many other aspects of my work in schools and elsewhere. The approach's emphasis on accepting, acknowledging, and accommodating client beliefs and positions has been immensely helpful in working with people from a variety of cultures and belief systems. This is an important consideration in light of the world's increasing multiculturalism.

Parent–School Conferences and Relationships

Parent–school conferences and relationships are enhanced when approached in a solution-focused manner. Parents are typically contacted by the school personnel only when their child is in trouble or struggling. Parents certainly need to be contacted in these circumstances. However, some parents actively avoid schools because most or all of the visits and conversations they have had with school personnel regarding their children have focused on "what's wrong."

The solution-focused emphasis on recognizing and empowering small changes might promote parent contact in other circumstances as well, such as when a student has a better day or week. Imagine your reaction as a parent if you were contacted by a teacher or counselor to inform you that your child has had a successful week in school. You might even be asked your opinion of how such improvements occurred, and what you and your child did differently that week to help bring about the change. As short and simple as this strategy sounds, it is not easy to do in the midst of the other pressing duties and "emergencies" faced by teachers, administrators, and counselors on a daily basis. Nonetheless, adopting a solution-focused philosophy may help schools move toward such practices in dealing with parents. Carlson, Hickman, and Horton (1992) recommend a solution-oriented approach to family–school meetings in which the focus is shifted from blaming each other for the student's problems to cooperating with each other to bring about solutions.

Classroom Management and Instruction

Solution-focused thinking can also be useful to teachers in classroom management and instruction. In analyzing students' math performance on a particular test or assignment, a teacher could ask them how they approached the problems that they got correct, in addition to inquiring about errors.

The concepts and strategies of solution-focused counseling can also assist teachers in resolving classroom behavior problems. For example, a teacher might ask a "difficult student" to present a short class report on the student's major hobby. This type of strategy increases the student's involvement in class and improves the teacher–student relationship, as well as acknowledging the student's unique talents and resources. Similarly, a teacher could ask the student's opinion of what might help turn things around for the better. As illustrated throughout this book, school professionals have nothing to lose and everything to gain by enlisting students as consultants on their own school problems. Students appreciate being asked about their opinions. Even if the student has no specific ideas for improving things, the question itself conveys respect and may enhance the teacher–student relationship. Ideas that incorporate the student's opinions are more likely to be acceptable and effective than ideas that ignore or exclude the student's input. Molnar and Lindquist (1989) present additional examples of how teachers can apply solution-focused strategies to classroom problems.

Parent and Teacher Training

Parent and teacher training can also be approached from a solution-focused perspective. Several years ago, I was asked to present a talk to parents of educationally disabled students on the topic of coping with the challenges of parenting. My plans to work on the presentation were blocked on several occasions, and I was considerably less prepared than I wanted to be as I stood before the 50 parents who attended the talk. I stumbled around for a few minutes without really saying anything. Then, in a moment of desperation, I asked the parents for their opinions on the most challenging aspects of their job, along with strategies for handling these challenges.

For the remainder of the hour, parents eagerly described various challenges and coping strategies associated with parenting educationally disabled students. I simply recorded their ideas on the board and occasionally asked questions to clarify their comments. Feedback from the parents who attended this session was very favorable, and included comments like "it was great to have a chance to talk instead of being talked to," and "I had no idea how many good ideas other parents had."

Teachers can be given similar opportunities to share effective teaching ideas and strategies in in-service training programs. The most effective in-service program that I participated in as a high school teacher was the one in which my social studies colleagues and I spent 2 hours sharing instructional and disciplinary strategies that worked particularly well for us. I was amazed at the number and quality of teaching ideas that were shared during this session. This was a great lesson on the importance of discovering and utilizing clients' own resources before looking outside for solutions. Just as it is important to ask an individual client what is already working in addressing the problem, training groups can be asked about what they are already doing effectively in the area for which they are being trained.

This book emphasized the application of solution-focused counseling to specific student-related problems. As noted in the examples above and in Box 12.1, the solution-focused approach is broadly applicable to various challenges and issues in middle and high schools.

> ### Box 12.1. More Than a Set of Strategies
> Solution-focused counseling is much more than a set of strate-gies for changing difficult school problems. It is a whole new way of thinking about people, problems, and schools.

JUMP IN AND HANG ON

When I played in a band, people would occasionally request songs that were unfamiliar to some or most of us in the group. If one or two band members knew the song fairly well, our bandleader Joe would look at the rest of us and say, "jump in and hang on." In most cases, it worked out pretty well. Over the years, Joe developed a keen sense of judgment regarding when to go for it and when to politely decline.

This story pertains to a caution regarding two extremes that occasionally befall us upon learning something new. The first extreme is to jump in with both feet and abandon practically everything we have been doing up to that point, including some things that have worked well. This response is incom-patible with the solution-focused emphasis on taking small steps and examin-ing what we are already doing successfully before trying something completely different.

The second and more common extreme of responding to a new counsel-ing approach is to be so cautious about trying it out that it is hardly worth learning in the first place. The only way to get better at doing anything is to do it. As with anything new, you may feel a bit uneasy and awkward the first few times you apply solution-focused strategies in your own work. However, you do not have to attend 20 workshops or read 20 books in order to start ap-plying some of the ideas and strategies of solution-focused counseling.

With these considerations in mind, I wish you well in putting this book to work where you work. Follow Joe's advice. *Jump in and hang on!*

A P P E N D I X A

Case Index

Numerous cases were presented throughout this book. This chart provides a quick reference to each case, the page on which it began, and a brief description.

Name/Case Title	Page Number	Description of Client/Problem/Solution
Janet ("An Introduction to Solution-Focused Counseling")	pg. 3	"Unmotivated" 11th-grade student; academic and discipline problems; worked within student's perspective instead of challenging it
Susan ("Clean More, Fight Less")	pg. 15	10th-grade student; "constant" fighting with father; discovered exceptions to the problem
Sandra ("The Making of an Impotent Technique")	pg. 18	10th grade student; poor study habits, "belligerent" attitude; parent offered various study strategies despite daughter's lack of interest
Patti ("When 'Not Knowing' is Smarter Than Knowing")	pg. 26	12th-grade student; declining grades, absenteeism, prior sexual abuse; listened more than talked
Paul ("The Student Who Refused to Read")	pg. 33	7th-grade student; refused to read; "looked at" maps instead of "reading" them
Jerry ("Tripping the Responsibility Trap")	pg. 36	6th-grade student; low grades and minimal homework completion; utilized parents' position to alter the evening homework routine
Tonia ("Growing Solutions From the Small Seeds of Success")	pg. 39	11th-grade student; increased conflicts with mother; utilized student's and mother's common interest in gardening

Continued on next page.

Continued from previous page.

Name/Case Title	Page Number	Description of Client/Problem/Solution
Raul ("What If Things Were Better, Raul?")	pg. 60	8th-grade student; truancy and minimal homework completion; "presupposed" positive changes and encouraged student to focus on the future instead of the past
Bobby ("Seeing What [and Who] You're Looking For")	pg. 64	4th-grade student; autistic-like behavior in the classroom; practitioner observed a different student and "saw" autistic-like behavior
Mario ("Mario's Meaningful Goal")	pg. 73	10th-grade student; thought principal and teachers were "out to get him"; renegotiated a goal that was relevant and meaningful to the student
Jolette ("Why Haven't You Given Up?")	pg. 81	12th-grade student; failing two classes, erratic attendance, chaotic home/family background; explored how student managed to "hang in there" and not give up
Jeff ("The Exceptional Quarter")	pg. 95	6th-grade student; referred for "behavior disability" assessment for talking out, oppositional behavior, peer difficulties; encouraged "more of" what worked during the "exceptional" second quarter of the school year
Group Application ("The Competent Test-Anxiety Group")	pg. 99	Five students in 10th & 11th grade; test anxiety problems; incorporated skill-building activities and solution-focused strategies
Joel ("The Student for Whom Nothing Was Going Right")	pg. 101	10th-grade student in advanced classes; declining grades, depression; used "formula first session task"
Bridgette ("Dorothy's Advice")	pg. 109	9th-grade student; "mouthing off" and minimal homework completion; utilized student's interest in old movies
Roy ("Sweeping the Sidewalk Twice")	pg. 111	8th-grade student; failing grades, cursing, refusal to do homework; encouraged student to apply "lawnmowing" skills to school work

Continued on next page.

Name/Case Title	Page Number	Description of Client/Problem/Solution
Dwayne ("Consulting Camus")	pg. 112	12th-grade student; had not completed graduation requirements; encouraged student to consider what his hero would advise him to do
Schoolwide Application ("Success Stories"); Larita	pg. 116	6th-grade student; improved her grade average from D to B; asked student how she managed to do this, and what advice she had for other students
Bruce ("The Lovesick Senior")	pg. 125	12th-grade student; agitated about recent breakup with girlfriend, "couldn't stop thinking about it"; recommended that student schedule "think times" during the week
Angela ("When Less is More")	pg. 128	7th-grade student; complained to teachers, counselor, and principal about how other students bothered her; acknowledged her concern instead of questioning or challenging it
William ("To Skip or Not To Skip, That Is the Question")	pg. 129	12th-grade student; skipped school, in jeopardy of not graduating; inquired about "disadvantages" of attending school
Jane ("Desperate and Developmental")	pg. 136	10th-grade student; declining grades, shame and depression about "nasty" phone behavior; offered a developmental interpretation
Zach ("Giving Them What They Want")	pg. 137	12th-grade student; oppositional and defiant behavior; proposed that defiant behavior may be "giving in" to teachers and principal
Jessica ("A Wake-Up Call From the Unconscious")	pg. 140	11th-grade student; nightmares, loss of concentration in school; suggested that nightmares were an indication of personal growth and progress
Steve ("Pervert or Parent Protector?")	pg. 142	6th-grade student; made obscene remarks and gestures to a teacher; invited student and grandparents to consider a more positive "function" of such behavior

Part One: The 9-Dot Problem (Watzlawick et al., 1974)

The nine dots in this puzzle can be connected using only four straight lines, drawn without taking your pencil off the paper. If you have not seen this puzzle before, take a few minutes to try to solve it. After you have tried to solve the puzzle, turn to the next page and check out the solution.

Part Two: The 9-Dot Solution (Watzlawick et al., 1974)

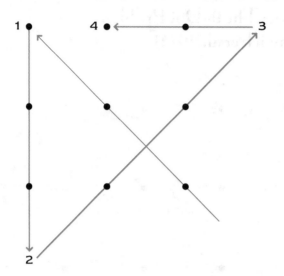

Very few people think of extending the straight lines beyond the dots, even though nothing about the task or the instructions prohibits doing so. Most people superimpose an imaginary square on the dots. The arbitrary and erroneous assumption that the lines cannot extend beyond the dots leads to "more of the same" solution attempts. The assumption that this is the only "reasonable" or "sensible" way to approach the problem inevitably leads to *failure and frustration*, the same two outcomes that befall teachers, parents, and counselors who are stuck in a pattern of applying more of the same ineffective strategies to a school problem.

You may have quickly recognized after just one or two tries that a solution to the puzzle was impossible, yet continued to apply the same solution theme, the superimposed square, over and over again. You probably varied specific aspects of your solution attempt such as the speed or intensity in which you applied it. However, the general theme of the solution remained the same, restricted by your assumption that you needed to stay within the square. In situations where people's attempts to resolve a school problem actually perpetuate it, solution opportunities are enhanced when counselors and clients step outside the limitations of existing solution attempts and "try something different."

Solution Identification Scale (S-Id) (Kral, 1988)

Name: _____ Date: _____ Rated by: _____

Please answer all questions. Beside each item, indicate the degree to which it occurs.

	Not at all	Just a little	Pretty much	Very much
1 Respectful to grown ups_____				
2 Able to make/keep friends_____				
3 Controls excitement _____				
4 Cooperates with ideas of others___				
5 Demonstrates ability to learn ____				
6 Adapts to new situations_____				
7 Tells the truth _____				
8 Comfortable in new situations ___				
9 Well behaved for age _____				
10 Shows honesty_____				
11 Obeys adults_____				
12 Handles stress well_____				
13 Completes what is started _____				
14 Considerate to others _____				
15 Shows maturity for age _____				
16 Maintains attention_____				
17 Reacts with proper mood_____				
18 Follows basic rules _____				
19 Settles disagreements peacefully _				
20 Gets along with brothers/sisters _				
21 Copes with frustration_____				
22 Respects rights of others _____				
23 Basically is happy_____				
24 Shows good appetite _____				
25 Sleeps OK for age _____				
26 Feels part of the family _____				

Continued on next page.

Continued from previous page.

	Not at all	Just a little	Pretty much	Very much
27 Stands up for self				
28 Is physically healthy				
29 Can wait for attention/rewards				
30 Tolerates criticism well				
31 Can share the attention of adults				
32 Is accepted by peers				
33 Shows leadership				
34 Demonstrates a sense of fair play				
35 Copes with distractions				
36 Accepts blame for own mistakes				
37 Cooperates with adults				
38 Accepts praise well				
39 Able to "think" before acting				

40   COMMENTS:

(Reproduced with permission from Brief Family Therapy Center.)

Quick Survey

Student: _____ Grade: _____ Date: _____

Teacher: _____

I have collected some information about this student's school problems and about factors that may be contributing to such problems. Your responses to the following questions will help me learn more about times and situations in which the student does better in your class. This might help us improve things by building on something the student is already doing successfully, even if they are not doing much of it at the current time.

1. Please list the things the student is currently doing (if only rarely), or has done, to succeed in this class?

   _____

   _____

   _____

2. Describe specific times and situations in your class when the student has done a little (or a lot) better than usual.

   _____

   _____

   _____

3. Based on the things you listed above, what might we start building upon in order to improve the student's performance in your class?

   _____

   _____

   _____

4. List any other information or comments that are important for me to consider in dealing with this situation.

   _____

   _____

   _____

THANK YOU FOR YOUR COOPERATION.

Documents to Help Students Clarify and Maintain Changes

The Consultant Club

This is to recognize

[Student's Name]

as an official member
of the Consultant Club.

The Consultant Club consists of students who have made important changes in school performance and who would be willing to serve as a consultant to [School Counselor] for advice on helping other students make changes.

_____, Consultant
Student's Name

_____, Club President
School Counselor

DOCUMENT #2

The Behavior Change Award
1997–1998 School Year

This award goes to

[Student's Name]

for making important, difficult changes
in school behavior during the
1997–1998 school year.

Principal

School Counselor

The Courage Award

In recognition of

[Student's Name]

for having the courage to make difficult, important changes in order to reach future career and life goals, and for remembering that any change worth making involves some bumps and slips along the way.

_____

School Counselor

DOCUMENT #4

Dear _____ :

I want to congratulate you for the recent changes you have made in your approach to school work and class behavior. I know that changes like this are difficult to make. I appreciate the courage it takes to keep on plugging instead of throwing the towel in and giving up when things get tough.

I was glad to hear that your teachers are treating you better. This makes sense to me. After all, it's hard to get on someone's case when they are cooperative in class and earning B's and C's instead of D's and F's.

I am curious what you have done to bring these grades up, and what it will take to continue doing this. The best ideas and suggestions that I have heard for helping students improve school work and behavior have come from students themselves—people like you who have actually made such improvements. Your ideas and suggestions will help me to help other students who are struggling with the same kinds of things that you were dealing with before you made these changes.

I congratulate you and look forward to our next discussion.

Sincerely,

School Counselor

DOCUMENT #5

Dear _____ :

I want to congratulate you on the improvements you have made in school behavior this year. I get real interested in how people make the kind of improvements you have made. It inspires me, and it gives me ideas for helping other people who are getting hassled in school like you used to.

I would like to meet with you to celebrate your success and to learn more about what you did to help bring about these changes. Please be thinking about what you have done to make things better, and what you are planning to do to keep things going well. I will contact you next week to set up a time when we can meet to discuss this.

Congratulations!

Sincerely,

School Counselor

The Solution-Focused Counseling Process

1. **Establish Cooperative, Change-Focused Relationships**

   - Adopt an *ambassador perspective* and convey your need for people to teach you about themselves and the problem.
   - *Match the client's language* (use words and phrases of the client).
   - *Match the client's position* (acknowledge client's beliefs and customership).
   - Use *presuppositional language* to convey hope and to promote a focus on the future.
   - *Collaborate* with clients throughout the counseling process.

2. **Define and Clarify Changeable Problems, Solution Attempts, Positions, Goals, Exceptions, and Other Client Resources**

   - Define the problem in *specific, behavioral terms* (videotalk).
   - Clarify *related circumstances* and *solution attempts* associated with the problem.
   - Develop goals that are *specific, small, positive*, and *meaningful*.
   - Clarify *client position* (beliefs and customership).
   - Identify and clarify *exceptions* to the problem.
   - Identify and clarify *other client resources*.

3. **Utilize Exceptions and Other Client Resources**

   - Encourage clients to *do "more of" the exception* by doing it more frequently and in different situations.
   - Encourage clients to *apply their own unique resources* (interests, talents, heroes, resilience, social supports) to the problem.

4. **If Useful Exceptions and Resources Are Not Identified, or if Clients Show a Preference for a Different Type of Intervention, Encourage A Change in the "Doing" or "Viewing" of the Problem**

   - In *changing the doing*, interrupt ineffective solution attempts and encourage clients to "do something different" in their performance of the problem or in their response to it.
   - In *changing the viewing*, suggest different yet plausible meanings or explanations of the problem.

5. **Evaluate and Maintain Progress**

   - *Evaluate* the progress of counseling by using scaling, paper-and-pencil measures, permanent products, and single-case evaluation designs.
   - Help clients *maintain* progress by empowering their intentions and plans to continue doing what works, blaming them for success, soliciting their suggestions and advice for others, clarifying the impact of change, preparing for relapse, using documents, and leaving the door open for follow-up contacts.

6. **Terminate Counseling**

   - Approach every session as the last.
   - Use goals as termination guidelines, and terminate when clients are "on track."
   - Offer follow-up contacts.

References

Alcoholics Anonymous. (1957). *Alcoholics Anonymous comes of age*. New York: Harper.

Ascher, L. M. (1989). Paradoxical intention and recursive anxiety. In L. M. Ascher (Ed.), *Therapeutic paradox* (pp. 93–136). New York: Guilford.

Bandura, A. (1977). Self-efficacy: Toward a unifying theory of behavior change. *Psychological Review, 84*, 191–215.

Barlow, D. H., Hayes, S. C., & Nelson, R. O. (1984). *The scientist-practitioner: Research and accountability in clinical and educational settings*. Elmsford, NY: Pergamon.

Barrios, B. A., & O'Dell, S. L. (1989). Fears and anxiety. In E. J. Mash & R. A. Barkley (Eds.), *Treatment of childhood disorders* (pp. 167–221). New York: Guilford.

Berg, I. K. (1991). *Family preservation: A brief therapy workbook*. London: Brief Therapy Press.

Bergan, J., & Tombari, M. (1976). Consultant skill and efficiency and the implementation and outcome of consultation. *Journal of School Psychology, 14*, 3–14.

Bigner, J. J. (1994). *Individual and family development: A life-span interdisciplinary approach*. Englewood Cliffs, NJ: Prentice-Hall.

Brigham, T. A. (1989). *Self-management for adolescents*. New York: Guilford.

Brooks, G. R. (1992). Gender-sensitive family therapy in a violent culture. *Topics in Family Psychology and Counseling, 1*, 24–36.

Bruner, J. (1987). Life as narrative. *Social Research, 54*, 11–32.

Budman, S. H., & Gurman, A. S. (1988). *Theory and practice of brief therapy*. New York: Guilford.

Cade, B., & O'Hanlon, W. H. (1993). *A brief guide to brief therapy*. New York: Norton.

Carkhuff, R. R.(1971). *The development of human resources*. New York: Holt, Rinehart, & Winston.

Carlson, C. I., Hickman, J., & Horton, C. B. (1992). From blame to solution: Solution-oriented family school consultation. In S. L. Christenson & J. C. Conoley (Eds.), *Home-school collaboration: Enhancing children's academic and social competence* (pp. 193–214). Silver Spring, MD: National Association of School Psychologists.

Carlson, J., & Lewis, J. (1993). *Counseling the adolescent: Individual, family and school interventions*. Denver: Love Publishing.

Coleman, E., & Remafedi, G. (1989). Gay, lesbian, and bisexual adolescents: A critical challenge to counselors. *Journal of Counseling and Development, 68*, 36–40.

Conoley, C. W., Ivey, D., Conoley, J. C., Scheel, M., & Bishop, R. (1992). Enhancing consultation by matching the consultee's perspectives. *Journal of Counseling and Development, 69*, 546–549.

Conoley, J. C. (1987). Strategic family intervention: Three cases of school-aged children. *School Psychology Review, 16,* 469–486.

Cormier, W. H., & Cormier L. S. (1991). *Interviewing strategies for helpers: Fundamental skills and cognitive behavioral interventions.* Pacific Grove, CA: Brooks/Cole.

de Shazer, S. (1984). The death of resistance. *Family Process, 23,* 11–21.

de Shazer, S. (1985). *Keys to solution in brief therapy.* New York: Norton.

de Shazer, S. (1988). *Clues: Investigating solutions in brief therapy.* New York: Norton.

de Shazer, S. (1991). *Putting difference to work.* New York: Norton.

de Shazer, S., Berg, I., Lipchik, E., Nunnally, E., Molnar, A., Gingerich, W., & Weiner-Davis, M. (1986). Brief therapy: Focused solution development. *Family Process, 25,* 207–222.

Duncan, B. L. (1989). Paradoxical procedures in family therapy. In M. L. Ascher (Ed.), *Therapeutic paradox* (pp. 310-348). New York: Guilford.

Dunst, C. J., & Trivette, C. M. (1987). Enabling and empowering families: Conceptual and intervention issues. *School Psychology Review, 16,* 443–456.

Durrant, M. (1995). *Creative strategies for school problems.* New York: Norton.

Dusek, J. B. (1991). *Adolescent development and behavior.* Englewood Cliffs, NJ: Prentice-Hall.

Elliott, S. N., Witt, J. C., Galvin, G., & Peterson, R. (1984). Acceptability of behavior interventions: Factors that influence teachers' decisions. *Journal of School Psychology, 22,* 353–360.

Erikson, E. (1968). *Identity: Youth, and crisis.* New York: W. W. Norton.

Erickson, M. H. (1954). Pseudo-orientation in time as a hypnotic procedure. *Journal of Clinical and Experimental Hypnosis, 2,* 161–283.

Fisch, R., Weakland, J. H., & Segal, L. (1982). *The tactics of change: Doing therapy briefly.* San Francisco: Jossey-Bass.

Forgatch M. S., & Patterson, G. R. (1989). *Parents and adolescents living together.* Eugene, OR: Castalia.

Frank, J. D., & Frank, J. B. (1991). *Persuasion and healing* (3rd ed.). Baltimore: Johns Hopkins Press.

Frankl, V. E. (1975). Paradoxical intention and deflection. *Psychotherapy: Theory, research and practice, 12,* 226–237.

Friedman, E. H. (1990). *Friedman's fables.* New York: Guilford.

Garfield, S. L. (1994). Research on client variables in psychotherapy. In A. E. Bergin & S. L. Garfield (Eds.), *Handbook of psychotherapy and behavior change* (pp. 190–228). New York: Wiley.

Garmezy, N. (1991). Resiliency and vulnerability to adverse outcomes associated with poverty. *American Behavioral Scientist, 34,* 416–430.

Goldenberg, I., & Goldenberg, H. (1994). *Counseling today's families* (2nd ed.). Pacific Grove, CA: Brooks/Cole.

Greenberg, L. S., Elliot, R. K., & Lietaer, G. (1994). Research on experimental psychotherapies. In A. E. Bergin & S. L. Garfield (Eds.), *Handbook of psychotherapy and behavior change* (pp. 190–228). New York: Wiley.

Gurman, A. S. (1977). Therapist and patient factors influencing the patient's perception of facilitative therapeutic conditions. *Psychiatry, 40,* 16–24.

Gutkin, T. B., & Curtis, M. J. (1990). School-based consultation: Theory, techniques and research. In T. B. Gutkin & C. R. Reynolds (Eds.), *The handbook of school psychology* (2nd ed., pp. 577–611). New York: Wiley.

Haley, J. (1973). *Uncommon therapy: The psychiatric techniques of Milton H. Erickson, M.D.* New York: Norton.

Haley, J. (Ed.) (1985). *Conversations with Milton H. Erickson, M.D. (Vol. 3): Changing children and families.* New York: Triangle Press.

Havighurst, R. J. (1970). *Developmental tasks and education.* New York: David McKay.

Hayes, S. B., & Melancon, S. M. (1989). Comprehensive distancing, paradox, and the treatment of emotional avoidance. In M. L. Ascher (Ed.), *Therapeutic paradox* (pp. 184–218). New York: Guilford.

Horowitz, M., Marmar, C., Weiss, D., DeWitt, K., & Rosenbaum, R. (1984). Brief psychotherapy of bereavement reactions: The relationship of process to outcome. *Archives of General Psychiatry, 41,* 438–448.

Howard, K., Kopta, M., Krause, M., & Orlinsky, D. (1986). The dose-effect relationship in psychotherapy. *American Psychologist, 41,* 149–164.

Hoyt, M. F., Rosenbaum, R., & Talmon, M. (1992). Planned single-session psychotherapy. In S. H. Busman, M. F. Hoyt, & S. Friedman, *The first session in brief therapy* (pp. 59–86). New York: Guilford.

Hubble, M. A., & Solovey, A. D. (1994). Ambassadorship in medical rehabilitation: A remedy for noncompliance. *Journal of Family Therapy, 13,* 67–76.

Jones, S. (1968). Instructions, self-instructions and performance. *Quarterly Journal of Experimental Psychology, 20,* 74–78.

Kazdin, A. E. (1980). Acceptability of alternative treatments for deviant child behavior. *Journal of Applied Behavior Analysis, 13,* 259–273.

Kazdin, A. E. (1994). *Behavior modification in applied settings.* Pacific Grove, CA: Brooks/Cole.

Kelly, G. A. (1955). *The psychology of personal constructs.* New York: Norton.

Kohut, H. (1980). Reflections. In A. Goldberg (Ed.), *Advances in self psychology* (pp. 473–554). New York: International Universities Press.

Koss, J., & Butcher, J. N. (1986). Research on brief psychotherapy. In S. L. Garfield & A. E. Bergin (Eds.), *Handbook of psychotherapy and behavior change* (3rd ed., pp. 627–670). New York: Wiley.

Koss, M. P., & Shiang, J. (1994). In A. E. Bergin & S. L. Garfield (Eds.), *Handbook of psychotherapy and behavior change* (pp. 664–700). New York: Wiley.

Kottler, J. A. (1991). *The compleat therapist.* San Francisco: Jossey-Bass.

Kowalski, K., & Kral, R. (1989). The geometry of solution: Using scaling techniques. *Family Therapy Case Studies, 4,* 59–66.

Kral, R. (1986). Indirect therapy in the schools. In S. de Shazer & R. Kral (Eds.), *Indirect approaches in therapy* (pp. 56–66). Rockville, MD: Aspen.

Kral, R. (1988). *Strategies that work: Techniques for solution in the schools.* Milwaukee, WI: Brief Family Therapy Center.

Kratochwill, T. R., & Bergan, J. R. (1990). *Behavioral consultation in applied settings: An individual guide.* New York: Plenum.

Kronenberger, W. G., & Meyer, R. G. (1996). *The child clinician's handbook.* Needham Heights, MA: Simon & Schuster.

Lambert, M. J. (1992). Implications of outcome research for psychotherapy integration. In J. C. Norcross & M. R. Goldfried (Eds.), *Handbook of psychotherapy integration* (pp. 94–129). New York: Basic Books.

Lawson, D. (1994). Identifying pretreatment change. *Journal of Counseling and Development, 72,* 244–248.

Lefton, L.A. (1994). *Psychology* (5th ed.). Needham Heights, MA: Allyn & Bacon.

Lewis, B. A., & Pucelik, F. (1982). Magic demystified: *Pragmatic guide to communication and change.* Portland, OR: Metamorphis Press.

Luborsky, L., Singer, B., & Luborsky, L. (1975). Comparative studies of psychotherapies: Is it true that "everybody has won and all must have prizes?" *Archives of General Psychiatry, 32*, 995–1008.

Marmar, C., Horowitz, M., Weiss, D., & Marziali, E.(1986). The development of the Therapeutic Alliance Rating System. In L. Greenberg & W. Pinsof (Eds.), *The psychotherapeutic process: A research handbook* (pp. 367–390). New York: Guilford.

Minuchin, S. (1974). *Families and family therapy.* Cambridge, MA: Harvard University Press.

Molnar, A., & Lindquist, B. (1989). *Changing problem behavior in schools.* San Francisco: Jossey-Bass.

Murphy, J. J. (1992). Brief strategic family intervention for school-related problems. *Family Therapy Case Studies, 7,* 59-71.

Murphy, J. J. (1994a, September). *Spotting the nose on our face: Students as intervention consultants.* Paper presented at the annual meeting of the Kentucky Association of Psychology in the Schools, Louisville, KY.

Murphy, J. J. (1994b). Working with what works: A solution-focused approach to school behavior problems. *The School Counselor, 42,* 59–65.

Murphy, J. J. (1996). Solution-focused brief therapy in the school. In S. D. Miller, M. A. Hubble, & B. L. Duncan (Eds.), *Handbook of solution-focused brief therapy: Research, theory, and practice.* San Francisco: Jossey-Bass.

Murphy, J. J., & Duncan, B. L. (1997). *Brief intervention for school problems.* New York: Guilford.

Newman, B. M., & Newman, P. R. (1991). *Development through life: A psychosocial approach.* Pacific Grove, CA: Brooks/Cole.

Nylund, D., & Corsiglia, V. (1994). Becoming solution-focused in brief therapy: Remembering something important we already knew. *Journal of Systemic Therapies, 13,* 5–12.

O'Hanlon, W. H. (1987). *Taproots: Underlying principles of Milton H. Erickson.* New York: Norton.

O'Hanlon, W. H., & Weiner-Davis, M. (1989). *In search of solutions: A new direction in psychotherapy.* New York: Norton.

O'Hanlon W. H., & Wilk, J. (1987). *Shifting contexts: The generation of effective psychotherapy.* New York: Guilford.

Orlinsky, D. E., Grawe, K., & Parks, B. K. (1994). Process and outcome in psychotherapy - noch einmal. In A. E. Bergin & S. L. Garfield (Eds.), *Handbook of psychotherapy and behavior change* (pp. 270–376). New York: Wiley.

Orlinsky, D. E., & Howard, K. I. (1986). Process and outcome in psychotherapy. In S. L. Garfield & A. E. Bergin (Eds.), *Handbook of psychotherapy and behavior change* (3rd ed., pp. 311–381). New York: Wiley.

Patterson, C. H. (1984). Empathy, warmth, and genuineness in psychotherapy: A review of reviews. *Psychotherapy, 21,* 431–438.

Patterson, C. H. (1989). Foundations for an eclectic psychotherapy. *Psychotherapy, 26,* 427–435.

Plas, J. (1986). *Systems psychology in the schools*. New York: Pergamon.

Reimers, T. M., Wacker, D. P., Cooper, L. J., & DeRaad, A. O. (1992). Acceptability of behavioral treatments for children: Analog and naturalistic evaluations by parents. *School Psychology Review, 21,* 628–643.

Reinking, R. H., Livesay, G., & Kohl, M. (1978). The effects of consultation style on consultee productivity. *American Journal of Community Psychology, 6,* 283–290.

Reuterlov, H., Lofgren, T., Nordstrom, K., & Ternstrom, A. (in press). What's better?: Clients' reports of change in second and subsequent sessions. *Brief Therapy.*

Ridley, C. R. (1995). *Overcoming unintentional racism in counseling and therapy: A practitioner's guide to intentional intervention*. Twin Oaks, CA: Sage.

Rogers, C. R. (1951). *Client-centered therapy*. Boston: Houghton Mifflin.

Rossi, E. L. (Ed.) (1980). *The collected papers of Milton Erickson*. New York: Irvington.

Rutter, M.(1985). Resilience in the face of adversity: Protective factors and resistance to psychiatric disorders. *British Journal of Psychology, 147,* 598–611.

Sarason, S. B. (1982). *The culture of the school and the problem of change* (2nd ed.). Boston: Allyn & Bacon.

Schave, D., & Schave, B. (1989). *Early adolescence and the search for self: A developmental perspective*. New York: Praeger.

Selekman, M. D. (1993). *Pathways to change: Brief therapy solutions with difficult adolescents*. New York: Guilford.

Shah, I. (1983). *The exploits of the incomparable Mulla Nasrudin*. London: Octagon Press.

Snyder, C. R., Irving, L. M., & Anderson, J. R. (1991). Hope and health. In C. R. Snyder & D. R. Forsyth (Eds.), *Handbook of social and clinical psychology: The health perspective* (pp. 285–305). Elmsford, NY: Pergamon.

Stokes, T. F., & Baer, D. M. (1977). An implicit technology of generalization. *Journal of Applied Behavior Analysis, 10,* 349–367.

Talmon, M. (1990). *Single-session therapy: Maximizing the effect of the first (and often only) therapeutic encounter*. San Francisco: Jossey-Bass.

Tomm, K. (1987). Interventive interviewing. *Family Process, 26,* 167–183.

Updyke, J. F., Melton, E. C., & Medway, F. (1981, April). *The effectiveness of school consultation: A meta-analysis perspective*. Paper presented at the annual meeting of the National Association of School Psychologists, Houston, TX.

Vargas, L. A., & Koss-Chioino, J. D. (Eds.) (1992). *Working with culture: Psychotherapeutic interventions with ethnic minorities*. San Francisco: Jossey-Bass.

Vernon, A. (1993). *Developmental assessment and intervention with children and adolescents*. Alexandria, VA: American Counseling Association.

Wallbridge, H. R., & Osachuk, A. G. (1995). *Therapy with adolescents*. In D. G. Martin & A. D. Moore (Eds.), *First steps in the art of intervention* (pp. 208–222). Pacific Grove, CA: Brooks/Cole.

Walter, J. L., & Peller, J. E. (1992). *Becoming solution-focused in brief therapy*. New York: Brunner/Mazel.

Watzlawick, P. (1984). *The invented reality*. New York: Norton.

Watzlawick, P. (1987). *The language of change*. New York: Norton.

Watzlawick, P., Weakland, J., & Fisch, R. (1974). *Change: Principles of problem formation and problem resolution*. New York: Norton.

Weiner-Davis, M., de Shazer, S., & Gingerich, W. (1987). Using pretreatment change to construct a therapeutic solution: An exploratory study. *Journal of Marital and Family Therapy, 13*, 359–363.

Werner, E. E., & Smith R. S. (1982). *Vulnerable but invincible: A study of resilient children*. New York: McGraw-Hill.

Wexler, D. B. (1991). *The adolescent self*. New York: Norton.

White, M., & Epston, D. (1990). *Narrative means to therapeutic ends*. New York: Norton.

Witt, J. C., & Elliott, S. N. (1985). Acceptability of classroom management strategies. In T. R. Kratochwill (Ed.), *Advances in school psychology* (Vol. 4, pp. 251–288). Hillsdale, NJ: Lawrence Erlbaum.

Worell, J., & Remer, P. (1992). *Feminist perspectives in therapy: An empowerment model for women*. New York: Wiley.

Zins, J. E., Maher, C. A., Murphy, J. J., & Wess, B. P. (1988). The peer support group: A means to facilitate professional development. *School Psychology Review, 10*, 138–146.

INDEX

0478